Proceedings of the Eleventh Annual Symposium sponsored by the Alumni and the Faculty of the Rutgers University Graduate School of Library Service

WOMEN IN LIBRARIANSHIP
MELVIL'S RIB SYMPOSIUM

MARGARET MYERS
MAYRA SCARBOROUGH
Editors

Bureau of Library and Information Science Research
Rutgers University Graduate School of Library Service
New Brunswick, New Jersey
1975

Library of Congress Cataloging in Publication Data

Main entry under title:
Women in librarianship: Melvil's rib symposium

(Issues in the Library and information sciences, no. 2)
    1.   2.
  I. Myers, Margaret, ed. II. Scarborough, Mayra, ed
III. Rutgers University, New Brunswick, N.J. Graduate
School of Library Service. III. Series.
ISBN 0-8135-0807-X

Published for the Graduate School of Library Science
by the Rutgers University Press, New Brunswick, New Jersey

Printed in the United States of America by
Quinn & Boden Company, Inc., Rahway, N.J.

CONTENTS

ACKNOWLEDGEMENTS

Each spring, the Graduate School of Library Service Alumni Association and the Graduate School of Library Service at Rutgers University jointly sponsor a symposium of interest to librarians. Past subjects have been collective bargaining, copyright, "changing" librarianship, library research, statewide library planning and the like.

In April, 1973, the eleventh annual event was on the topic, "Women in Librarianship: Melvil's Rib Symposium." It was felt that the papers and discussion which followed should be published as the second book in the Rutgers series "Issues in the Library and Information Sciences."

Many people contributed both in arranging and conducting the actual symposium and in the preparation of this book. These persons should be acknowledged and thanked for their efforts. First of all, the four panelists contributed not only on the symposium day but later in preparing the copy for publication. In addition, a number of special guests at the symposium added to the dicussion at lunch and during the microphone repartee.

The 1973 conference committee was composed of members of the Executive Board of the Rutgers University Library School Alumni Association with assistance from several faculty and staff members of the Library School. The many details of the symposium arrangements were handled by the University Alumni Relations Office, while the Series Editor helped with advice and assistance in completing the publication.

We thank all of them.

Margaret Myers
Mayra Scarborough
Editors

Acknowledgements

George J. Lukac, *Assistant Director of Alumni Relations, Rutgers University*

Henry Voos, *Series Editor, Rutgers Graduate School of Library Service*

GRADUATE SCHOOL OF LIBRARY SERVICE
ALUMNI ASSOCIATION BOARD, 1973

Leonie M. Brinkema, *President*
    Morris County Library
    Whippany, N.J.

Mayra Scarborough, *President Elect and Symposium Chairperson*
    Business Information Center
    Hoffmann-La Roche, Inc.
    Nutley, N.J.

Diane S. Sederoff, *Secretary*
    Rutgers University Library
    New Brunswick, N.J.

Margaret Jiuliano, *Newsletter Editor*
    Newark State College Library
    Union, N.J.

Sally Sullivan, *Alumni Magazine Reporter*
    Madison Public Library
    Madison, N.J.

Joe Scorza, *Personnel Liaison Officer*
    Rutgers Research Information Services Bureau
    New Brunswick, N.J.

Shirley Bolles, *Past President*
    Rutgers Library of Science and Medicine
    New Brunswick, N.J.

Helen Montgomery, *GSLS Representative, Alumni Federation, Board of Governors*
    Berkeley Heights Library
    Berkeley Heights, N.J.

Richard L. Strickler, *GSLS Representative, Alumni Federation, Board of Governors*
    Toms River High School North
    Toms River, N.J.

GRADUATE SCHOOL OF LIBRARY SERVICE
STAFF REPRESENTATIVES

Thomas H. Mott, Jr., *Dean*

R. Kay Maloney, *Faculty Liaison*

Margaret Myers, *Faculty Symposium Consultant*

Ernest DeProspo, *Faculty Symposium Consultant*

Peggy Hoydis, Diane Katz, Margaret Koye Avalos, Phyllis Pohl,
    Office Staff

SPECIAL GUESTS

Kenneth F. Duchac, *Director*
    Brooklyn Public Library
    Grand Army Plaza,
    Brooklyn, N.Y.
Janet D. Bailey, *Editor*
    Special Libraries
    235 Park Avenue South
    New York, N.Y.
Hope Tillman Nagy, *Editorial Reporter*
    New Directions for Women in New Jersey
    Rider College Library
    Trenton, N.J.
Patricia Glass Schuman, *Editor*
    Library/Education Book Program
    R. R. Bowker Company
    1180 Avenue of the Americas
    New York, N.Y.
Ted Slate, *Librarian*
    Newsweek Inc.
    444 Madison Avenue
    New York, N.Y.
Helen Tuttle, *Preparations Department*
    Princeton University Library
    Princeton, N.J.

INTRODUCTION

There are some who question whether the status of women in the library profession is a major issue. A survey of library literature, however, shows an increase in the factual data available regarding differences between men and women in salaries, promotional patterns and other professional situations. There are local library groups which are examining the status of women in their own libraries and organizing to improve their employment situations. On the state and national level, conference programs and workshops at library association meetings have dealt with various aspects of sex discrimination, affirmative action policies, sexism in children's materials and the like. A program on the welfare of women in librarianship at the American Library Association annual conference in Las Vegas in 1973 drew over one thousand persons. At least one library school has introduced a course on women in librarianship; at others, a number of students are writing papers on the topic. Active since 1970, the American Library Association Social Responsibilities Round Table Task Force on Women has become a growing national coalition of women which has its own newsletter, carries out surveys and other projects, and conducts information and business meetings at the annual Association conferences. In 1974, they held an intensive two-day preconference on the topic of "Women in a Woman's Profession: Strategies," when a nationwide network of women to eradicate sex discrimination in libraries was formed. A network SHARE (Sisters Have Resources Everywhere) will co-ordinate regional and national efforts and resources to correct sexism through affirmative action programs, career development projects, studies of library education discrimination and participation in unions.

The Canadian Library Association also has an active women's group which organizes conference programs, conducts research and issues a newsletter.

In organizing the Rutgers symposium, the planning committee
felt that the topics discussed should include an overview of the past
and present status of women within the library profession, a look at
some of the sociological and psychological factors which have an
influence on this profession as well as other aspects of society, and
a brief discussion of legal and other steps which could be taken to
overcome sex discrimination. The three speakers, Anita R. Schiller, Carolyn W. Sherif and Herman Greenberg deal with these
aspects, while the panel moderator, Harold Wooster, provides an
introduction via a fable.

The presentation by Anita Schiller will shed some light on the
meaning of ''Melvil's Rib'' for those for whom the meaning is not
apparent. The audience questions and comments at the end point
up the varied concerns of individuals about their own uncertainties
and library situations as well as more generalized concerns about
discrimination on an institutional basis and male-female relationships in a work environment. Noting the lack of male representation in the audience, some audience members felt that men generally did not consider the symposium topic to be a serious, professional concern or else were threatened by it. However, the audience in general seemed to feel that discrimination existed, that
there were serious problems which existed and that the profession
should address itself to dealing with them.

It is hoped that this publication will be used in generating further
discussion and action among librarians regarding the problems we
face in our work and in our relations with each other as males and
females. The speakers have outlined the problems and suggested
some courses of action; they point out that the problems of discrimination in the library profession and in society in general are
not necessarily individual problems but need to be confronted on
an institutional scale through the actions of many people, men and
women, working together.

HAROLD WOOSTER

Chief, Research and Development Branch, Lister Hill National Center for Biomedical Communication, National Library of Medicine, spins his second fable here. The first, called "Machina Versatilis—A Modern Fable," carried the following disclaimer, when it was presented at the Special Libraries Association's annual convention in New York City in 1967: "Since this divertissement is so obviously science fiction, it is supererogatory to point out that any resemblance to Designers, Information Systems or Computers, Living or Dead, is completely coincidental."

A.B. magna cum laude, *Syracuse University; Ph.D. University of Wisconsin; other desiderata—such as Phi Beta Kappa Key—can be uncovered by browsing through* American Men of Science, Who's Who in the South and Southeast, Leaders in American Science, Dictionary of International Biography 1967, The Two Thousand Men of Achievement.

HOW THE LIBRARY CHANGED
ITS SPOTS—AN AIN'T SO STORY

Many eons away, O Best Beloved, there was a large, dank, dim cave inhabited by a tribe of large, fierce, hairy Guardians. They wore dark robes that did not show the dirt; they never bathed, they never shaved. They were too busy Guarding their sacred Treasures from the periodic raids of the Bandar-Log—strange chattering simian creatures who dwelt in the shattered red brick Georgian ruins of something they called "durms." From time to time one of these little anthropoids would steal past the Guardians into the back of the Cave and try to make away with one of the Treasures clutched in a prehensile paw. Needless to say, they were severely beaten as a lesson to their fellows. The best time for raiding was during the fifteen-minute intervals, at ten in the morning and three in the afternoon, when the Guardians would sit down, grasp a mug of hot water and stare at the wall. The ritual was thought to have a religious significance—only the name survives, "kafe-brick."

These Treasures, rank in serried rank across the back of the Cave, were housed in glass-fronted shrines, bearing the cabalistic symbol, "Globe-Wernicke." Through the glass, purpled with age, clouded with the grime of centuries, could be seen the Treasures, gold letters still dully gleaming, bound in full calf, half calf, and a peculiarly nasty fabric the Guardians had been taught to call "buckrum."

The Guardians and their Treasures were very happy together. Once a week, women from the neighboring village would approach with their offerings—a cereal mixture made of oats, brown sugar, wheat germ, flaked or shredded coconut, sesame seed or sunflower seed, chopped walnuts, pecans. peanuts or unchopped raisins (the week they chopped the raisins is still marked in black in the

Guardians' annuals), salad oil, honey, vanilla extract—all neatly packaged in nonbiodegradable plastic jugs, one of the few remainders, together with aluminum beer cans, of an earlier civilization. Once a week they would take the empty jugs back to the village to be refilled.

These village women were a bleak, drab lot as they walked up the hill to the Cave—long straight hair, no makeup (well, perhaps a trace of eye-shadow), skirts half-way between knee and ankle, feet shod in clumsy contraptions of cloth and rubber named after a long forgotten game—"tennishuz."

The tradition of centuries kept the women at the threshold of the Cave. They would deposit their jugs and withdraw; the Guardians would then pick up the jugs and carry them through tortuous passages to the Refectory.

And then one day the Devil discovered the Cave. He wore one of his conventional disguises, the three-button uniform of the Industrial Engineer. He briefed his hosts one evening after a frugal (but very healthy) meal and pointed out that they had been committing Sins against the Doctrines of Engineering. Now the Guardians had only tattered remnants of formal religion—about the only thing left was an Icon, hanging over the Treasures. It read:

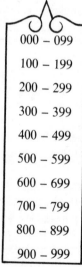

The Rituals of the Cave decreed that formal obeisance be made to this tablet before removing or replacing a Treasure from a shrine; it was usually referred to as the Ten Commandments.

With the aid of slip-scrolls, extracted from a slim black attaché case, and a clever chromium-plated collapsible pointer, the Devil told the Guardians of their Doctrinal Sins—not only were they guilty of Double Handling of Materials but, even worse, they had been Operating below Grade Level and not Delegating Responsibility. Time spent in carrying jugs could be better spent in Guarding Treasures.

Changes were immediately instituted. The women were asked to carry the jugs back to the Refectory. And having introduced women to the Cave, the Devil went happily on his way. The Inevitable Forces of Nature could now take over.

At first, nothing happened. Then the women began to ask why it always had to be so dark in the Cave. "Because it's always been dark in here," was the very proper answer they got. One of the women noticed thin rays of light coming through one wall of the Cave, another saw that a large boulder was blocking a hole in the wall, a third, more brash than the others, asked the Chief Guardian what would happen if the boulder were removed? "Impossible, it's much too big to move," she was told. "But you're so big and strong, it would be easy for you." This worked, as it always has, and the boulder went tumbling down the mountainside. Sunlight and fresh air streamed in—almost too much sunlight and fresh air. On their next weekly trip the women brought willow withes and strips of curiously decorated fabric, the withes fed through loops at the top of the fabric, and wedged in place in cracks at the top of the aperture. In one short week the women had invented windows, window curtains and the Systems Approach.

The Treasures were housed, as all proper Treasures should be, by size-proud folios next to folios, quartos by quartos, octavos by octavos, the dumpy twelves huddled together. Once or twice a week the Guardians would walk up and down in front of the Shrines, carefully removing a Treasure here and there, and carry the pile over to a long table. Opening Treasure after Treasure, they would scribble furiously on scraps of paper, then close the Treasures and restore them to their proper places in the Shrines.

"What are they doing?" said wide-eyed Drusilla.

"They are making Literature Searches."

"But why do they have to go to so many different Shrines?"

"Because Treasures on one subject come in many different sizes, and have to be stored in Shrines of the proper shelf-spacing."

"But wouldn't it be simpler to store Treasures on the same subject together? That way you wouldn't have to do so much walking, and would have more time free to Guard your Treasures against the Bandar-Log."

"How would we know which Treasure went with which?"

"That's easy. You make little marks on the backs of the Treasures dealing with the same subject, and store Treasures with the same little marks together."

Subject Classification and Shelving had been invented. Far away, the Devil chuckled, as the Guardians split into furious camps, some arguing that the marks on the Sacred Icon should be used, others busily rediscovering analytico-synthetic faceted classifications. These latter ones tended to sit in the lotus position for hours, murmuring the mystic phrase, "APUPA," or chanting, "Personality, Matter, Energy, Space and Time." While they were chanting, the Decimal Drones kept busy reclassifying the Treasures.

While all this was going on, a delegation of women waited on the Chief Guardian. They explained to him that it was an awfully long walk up from the village, that asking them to carry the jugs back to the Refectory made the walk even longer, and that it would be nice if they could have a place to sit down and rest before they started back. A vacant alcove was found, and a few scraps of discarded furniture, even a sign to hang over the door:

> ⅃ YE STAFF LOUNGE

A fire, a pot, and some water were the next modest requests. Strange fragrances began to waft forth as the women brought the water to a rolling bubbling boil and added pinches of a dried herb they brought with them in little bags. Some of the younger Guardians even became addicted to this brew and spent time at the entrance to the Staff Lounge that should have been spent Guarding or Literature Searching.

Meanwhile, back in the Main Reading Room, the women continued to observe. A Guardian would approach a Shrine, remove a Treasure, open it to the Title Page, look at it, and return the Treasure.

"Why are they doing that?"

"They are Verifying the author, the title and the publisher."

"But wouldn't it be simpler to write all those things down on a piece of paper? That way you would just have to look at the piece of paper, instead of lifting those big heavy treasures. And why not have the pieces of paper all the same size, so you could keep them in little boxes?"

The Card Catalog and Descriptive Cataloging had been invented.

Much of the rest of this story is lost in the mists of futurity. We know that women had been introduced into the Cave, that the tasks of handling and Guarding the Treasures had been changed from physical to intellectual. We have only another tattered piece of paper brought back by the Time Probe. Internal evidence, and the small neat uncials, date it from a time several centuries after this manuscript. It reads:

"Many eons away, O Best Beloved, there was a bright, cool airy cave inhabited by a tribe of fierce long-haired Guardians. Once a week men from the neighboring village would approach with their offerings. . . ."

Acknowledgments

Stimulus for this paper was provided by Mayra Scarborough, who found that "But you're so clever" works as well as "But you're so big and strong" has always worked. Inspiration, however, has been provided by two wives, Marcia and the present incumbent, Alice, three daughters, Ann-Sargent, Pamela and Katharine, the two latest of a series of female cats, Bagheera and M'Toto, various coworkers, Johanna, Jehane and Jinnet, Kipling's "The Cat that Walked by Himself" and Walter M. Miller's "A Canticle for Leibowitz."

ANITA R. SCHILLER

Reference Bibliographer, University of California, San Diego, who previously held an appointment at the Library Research Center of the University of Illinois Graduate School of Library Service.

During 1967–68 Ms. Schiller was Project Director of a U.S. Office of Education grant for a study called "Characteristics of Professional Personnel in College and University Libraries." This resulted in a well-acclaimed report published by the Illinois State Library in 1969 (their Research Series: No. 16). Chapters for four books in the library field, many published articles and reviews and a long list of seminar-conference-institute presentations add to her stature as a strong and authoritative voice on "Sex and Library Careers."

ANITA R. SCHILLER

SEX AND LIBRARY CAREERS

Melvil Dewey launched the first professional library school in the United States at Columbia College in 1887. On opening day women students were in the majority. The school closed a short time thereafter, and that was why. Charged by the Columbia trustees with countermanding official policy when he allowed women to enroll, Dewey was found guilty and forced to resign. Although the school closed as a result, Dewey began anew at Albany and was vindicated many years later when Columbia University's library school reopened as a coeducational institution in 1926. Dewey spoke at the reopening.

There were probably several reasons for Dewey's conviction that the profession should be open to women; dedication to equal opportunity was one of them. But there were other reasons and these may have been more significant.

Mae West isn't a reference librarian but she has a lot of answers. When someone came up to her one day and said, "Goodness, what a beautiful mink stole," she replied: "Goodness—my dear—has nothing to do with it." Similarly, Dewey's recruitment of women into librarianship was based on some very tangible and practical reasons.

For one thing, the field at that time was called "Library Economy." And with good reason: library resources were scarce, and the need to "educate and elevate," as Dewey put it, was great. Operating under severe financial constraints, the library profession sought all possible ways to maximize its limited resources. The employment of women was one way to do this.

Other librarians joined with Dewey in urging women to enter this developing field. As early as 1877, only a year after the founding of the American Library Association, Justin Winsor, addressing a librarians' conference in London, explained why women were wanted:

In American libraries we set a high value on women's work. They soften our atmosphere, they lighten our labour, they are equal to our work, and for the money they cost . . . they are infinitely better than equivalent salaries will produce of the other sex. For from £100 to £160 a year we can command our pick of the educated young women whom our Colleges for Women are launching forth upon our country . . . women with a fair knowledge of Latin and Greek, a good knowledge of French and German, and who do not stagger at the acquisition of even Russian, if the requirements of catalogue service make that demand. It is to these Colleges for Women, like Vassar and Wellesley, that the American library system looks confidently for the future.[1]

Winsor's explanation was straightforward. By employing women—and notice the stress on their educational qualifications—the profession got more for its money. It is quite clear, however, that this arrangement was not seen as exploitative. On the contrary, it was seen to be in the best interest of women themselves. Librarianship, in fact, has since been regarded as one of the few professions where women have equal opportunity. Among the public at large, and among librarians, women's predominance has been taken to mean women's equality.

Yet if this profession opened its doors to women when most other professions closed women out, this was not simply due to an affirmative-action outlook. The open-door policy stemmed instead from a basic lack of support for librarianship itself. By recruiting women and utilizing a marginal labor force, a marginal profession was able to stretch its limited resources and advance its own development. Because women were barred from employment in almost every other profession, they could be attracted to this one on less than equal terms. Inequality, then, was the basic condition for women's employment as librarians. In this sense, libraries employed women to advantage by capitalizing on the segregation which excluded them from other fields.

In our enlightened times the condition of inequality remains. Librarianship is still, overall, a marginal activity, and occupational segregation still exists. Today, for example, 90 percent of all physicians, 95 percent of all lawyers and 98 percent of all engineers are men. Yet 97 percent of all nurses, 84 percent of all elementary school teachers and 82 percent of all librarians are women.[2] Along with social work and dietetics, where women also predominate, these few fields account for the majority of all women professional and technical workers. If we include secondary school teaching, we find that nearly two out of every three women professional workers in the United States are employed in only six fields. The 1970 *Manpower Report of the President* points out that common characteristics of those professions which are staffed predominantly by women "include their service orientation and heavy concentration in the nonprofit sectors of the economy."[3] Another common characteristic is low salaries. These fields supply needed public services, but they rarely enjoy the rewards common to the profit-bearing sectors. Yet if the predominance of women among librarians does not signify equality, this is something we've just begun to discover.

Current Status

There are three key indicators of women's status within the various occupations. The first concerns salaries; the second, job levels; and the third, job type. Whatever occupation we examine, these indicators show very consistently that women earn lower salaries than men, that women are concentrated in the lower level jobs, and that women tend to be segregated into those positions that are typed for the female sex.

These patterns are pervasive throughout the occupational structure. That women who worked full-time the year round in 1970 earned only 59 percent of what their male counterparts made is only one summary illustration.[4] That women have accepted their alleged inferiority in the world of work only serves to show how deep these patterns are.

A recent news story from Great Britain reports, for example, that when an executive job for women was advertised at a salary of $8,400, no one applied. When the same job was readvertised at $3,360, the applications poured in.[5] As this incident illustrates, occupational inequality between the sexes takes subtle and complex forms. It is not due simply to the willful discrimination of prejudiced males. We are dealing here with a set of institutional conditions—social, economic and cultural. These conditions have fostered occupational segregation. They have confined women's work opportunities to certain fields and restricted women's opportunities for advancement in all of them.

What do the three basic indicators of women's status in librarianship show? Let us look at salary levels first. In April, 1971, *American Libraries* published the results of a salary survey of ALA members. The median salary for men was $14,171; for women it was $10,874. Differentials were reported for all levels of education and for all job categories. Differences in salary levels of men and women have also been reported in surveys of special librarians, public librarians, academic librarians, law librarians, state librarians and federal librarians.

A study of library science doctorates published in 1970 reported a median salary for men of $18,300, for women, $13,800.[6] An earlier survey of academic librarians found that salary differentials between men and women widened with experience. Among those with less than five years of professional experience, the median salary for women was 92 percent of the men's; but among those with twenty or more years of experience, women earned only 70 percent as much as their male counterparts.[7] Examining promotional patterns for women in a single large university library, a 1971 affirmative action report measured the hypothetical salary loss to the woman librarian over a twenty-year period. The loss was quite substantial. It amounted to $24,000.[8]

Let's turn now to job levels. Here we find that women are

concentrated in the lower echelon positions, and at the top they are scarcely represented at all. Although women constitute 82 percent of the library profession, they hold only 39 percent of the top administrative posts in the largest public libraries (those serving populations of 100,000 or more); only 37 percent of these positions in the largest special libraries and information centers (those with staffs of ten or more); and only 8 percent of these posts in the largest academic libraries (those in institutions with enrollments of 3,000 or more).[9] In fact, as the size of the library increases, women's representation tapers off. In public library systems serving populations of 100,000 to 400,000, women hold 40 percent of the directorships. In the very largest public libraries serving populations of 750,000 or more, women's representation drops to 10 percent.[10]

The higher the career ladder ascends, the less likely it is that women will be on it. This occurs across the profession as a whole and also in individual libraries. In the Library of Congress, we might expect a more equitable distribution of the two sexes at each rung of the ladder, but instead at each successive step upward the percentage of women diminishes. At the GS-9 level, which is the starting point for those with a library degree, 54 percent of all positions are held by women; but at the higher GS-16 through GS-18 levels the figure is 4 percent. Only two of these fifty-five "supergrade" positions are held by women. There are three positions above this level, and women hold none of them.[11]

The career patterns of men and women librarians differ not only by job level but also by type of library. Just as in other professions, where women are more likely to enter certain subfields than others—as women doctors, for example, are more likely to be pediatricians than surgeons—women librarians are more likely to work in school libraries, where about nine out of every ten librarians are women, than in libraries of other types, and least so in academic libraries, where the corresponding figure is just over six out of ten. However, if work in each type of library is ranked by the level of esteem it is accorded, the ranking is ordered precisely in reverse. In that case, academic libraries are at the top and school libraries at the bottom.[12]

Library Careers—The Double Standard

Back in the nineteen forties, Alice Bryan did a major study of the public librarian. Bryan concluded that there were two separate career structures for librarians—one for the minority, who were men, and another, confined within much lower limits, for the majority, who were women. These two separate career structures have existed for a long time, but they have been integrated so closely into the total environment that they have been all but invisible. They have seemed, in fact, to be a part of the natural order. Today, as we begin to recognize that other perspectives are possible, these two separate structures begin to become more distinct. Looking back, we can see now that not only salary levels but even the nature of library work have been governed by two separate sets of rules—one for women, and another for men.

Recruitment appeals are illustrative, for they emphasize different career opportunities, depending on which sex is being addressed. Here is Dewey describing librarianship as a profession for college-bred women, in an address to the Association of Collegiate Alumnae in 1886:

In the library profession, the best work will always be done on the moral plane. . . . The selfish considerations of reputation, or personal comfort, or emolument are all secondary. . . .[13] There is absolutely no attraction for salary hunters.[14]

Advice to men, at a somewhat later date, went this way:

I rather hesitate to thrust the dollars and cents sign into the foreground but it makes if not a high, at least an insistent appeal.[15]

We should note here, too, that the profession was never supported adequately enough to pay decent salaries to either sex. But while salaries were seen as at least a reasonable interest for men, women were advised to be above this concern. Women were instructed by Melvil in other ways as well:

There is no room for those who wish to take up library work simply because they fancy it to be easier and more agreeable to one who is fond of books and cultivated society. . . . In fact, the work is not easy . . . and though surrounded constantly by thousands of books . . . there is hardly any occupation which gives so little opportunity to read. Our traditional motto is: "The librarian who reads is lost." Of course, I am speaking now of working hours.[16]

To men, however, the matter was presented like this:

[The most potent appeal] is the call of the book. To the man of scholarly tastes and habits, books in themselves yield a unique pleasure.[17]

But whether the man of scholarly tastes and habits was to cultivate them during or after working hours evidently was not an issue.

Another reason for men to join the profession seems to have been even more compelling than the call of the book. This was the call of career advancement. Using unequal opportunity as the basis of the appeal, the call to men urged them to join the profession because their sex gave them a career advantage. One of the numerous examples of this discriminatory appeal appeared in a section of the New York State Library School's 1907 annual report called *Men in Library Work*. The report points out that women outnumbered men at the previous year's ALA conference, but of those who were registered as chief librarians the men outnumbered the women. "These figures," states the report, "furnish the reason why there is great promise and opportunity for good men in library work." It goes on to add: "Men have probably always been preferred for the chief positions. . . ." [18]

Standard recruitment practices have supported an arrangement where the doors to certain positions have been open to men but closed to women. Although want-ads which designate sex are now illegal, until recently they were commonplace, and they have left their mark. Here are a few of them:

Director of Technical Processing Center. The Director will plan, establish, organize and administer the center. *He* will review . . .

Head, Science Library. Major academic research library desires man. . . . Must be scholarly and able to communicate with scientists . . .

Administrative services librarian needed by suburban library system. *He* will help develop and carry out. . . . *He* may investigate specific problems . . .

Head, Undergraduate Library. Major university desires innovative young *man*.

(Italics added)

These ads appeared in *Wilson Library Bulletin,* January, 1968, *Library Journal,* January, 1969, and *ACRL News,* December, 1969, and February, 1970.[19] These illustrations make it quite clear that library jobs have not been open equally to all. They have been classified by sex, and the classification system has been effective. If certain jobs were labelled for men, the bulk of them were stamped for women, who were wanted to perform a subordinate role. In this sense women were seen to be uniquely suited to the hierarchical organization of large libraries.

Frank Hill, who was chief librarian at the Newark Free Public Library soon after it was established, examined how a library staff should be organized and managed. Writing in *Library Journal* in 1897, he began as follows:

It is quite essential that there should be only one head, and that *he* should know *his* business. . . . The librarian must "keep at" his assistants if *he* wishes to secure system and order. . . . The ideal assistant should be willing to do whatever is asked of *her*. She should be always courteous and polite, good-natured and obedient, accurate, systematic and orderly, prompt and regular, attentive and faithful, enthusiastic. . . .[20]

(Italics added)

Hill offered some other pointers for properly instructing female subordinates. The main emphasis of his discourse was on rules. Quoting from the *Public Library Handbook,* he stated: "If the library authorities have established a certain way of doing a thing . . . determine to understand it thoroughly and follow it faithfully. The end and aim of every system is order and economy." He goes on to explain: "It is better to submit to what may seem stringent rules than to take the government in one's own hands. . . . In short, obedience is one of the chief foundation stones of the library organization." [21]

But today libraries and librarians are finding that the old rules don't work. Hierarchical structures of library organization are being challenged by demands for professional autonomy, and librarians are beginning to assert the belief that government should be in their own hands. If, as a marginal profession, librarianship recruited women because they could be employed at low cost, this is no longer accepted as a reasonable arrangement. If the old rules were based on a double standard for library careers, then the old rules need to be changed. It is up to women and men librarians together to change them.

Notes

1. Conference of Librarians, *Transactions and Proceedings of the Conference of Librarians Held in London, October 1877* (London: Trübner, 1878), p. 177.

2. *Economic Report of the President, Together with the Annual Report of the Council of Economic Advisors* (Washington, D.C.: U.S. Government Printing Office, 1973), pp. 155–56.

3. U.S. Department of Labor, *Manpower Report of the President* (Washington, D.C.: U.S. Government Printing Office, 1970), p. 185.

4. U.S. Bureau of the Census, *Current Population Reports* (Washington, D.C.: U.S. Government Printing Office, 1971) (P-60, No. 80), p. 129.

5. Jules Arbose, "British Women Making Small Progress on Pay Equality with Men," *New York Times,* January 15, 1973, p. 43.

6. Raymond L. Carpenter and Patricia A. Carpenter, "The Doctorate in Librarianship and an Assessment of Graduate Library Education," *Journal of Education for Librarianship* 11:17 (Summer, 1970).

7. Anita R. Schiller, *Characteristics of Professional Personnel in College and University Libraries* (Research Series, No. 16) (Springfield, Illinois: Illinois State Library, 1969). (ED 020 766), p. 86.

8. University of California, Berkeley, Library Affirmative Action Program for Women Committee, *A Report on the Status of Women Employed in the University of California, Berkeley, with Recommendations for Affirmative Action,* 1971. (Processed) (ED 066 163)

9. These figures are drawn from three of the library manpower studies by Mary Lee Bundy and Paul Wasserman, University of Maryland, School of Library and Information Services: *The Academic Library Administrator and His Situation,* 1970 (ED 054 796), pp. 77–79. *The Administrator of a Special Library or Information Center and His Situation,* 1970

(ED 054 799), pp. 73–76. *The Public Library Administrator and His Situation,* 1970 (ED 054 797), pp. 79–80.

10. Raymond L. Carpenter and Kenneth D. Shearer, "Sex and Salary Survey: Selected Statistics of Large Public Libraries in the United States and Canada," *Library Journal* 97:3682-84 (November 15, 1972).

11. "Library of Congress Personnel Statistics," *FLC Newsletter, Federal Library Committee,* no. 67: 17 (September, 1972).

12. J. H. Walters, *Image and Status of the Library and Information Services Field* (Washington, D.C.: U.S. Office of Education, Bureau of Research, 1970). (ED 045 130), p. 8.

13. Melvil Dewey, *Librarianship as a Profession for College-Bred Women* (Boston: Library Bureau, 1886), p. 19.

14. *Ibid.,* p. 22.

15. "Librarianship for College Men," *Reserve Weekly,* December 21, 1909. In New York State Library School, *Librarianship: An Uncrowded Calling* (Albany, New York: New York State Education Department, 1911), p. 11.

16. Dewey, *Librarianship as a Profession,* p. 22.

17. Dewey, "Librarianship for College Men," p. 11.

18. Annual Report of the New York State Library School for 1907, pp. 216–17. In New York State Library School, *Librarianship: An Uncrowded Calling* (Albany, New York: New York State Education Department, 1911), p. 7.

19. Quoted in a memorandum on Activities 1969–70, to the ALA LAD/PAS Committee on Economic Status and Fringe Benefits, from its Subcommittee Investigating Sexual Discrimination. (Processed, n.d.)

20. Frank P. Hill, "Organization and Management of a Library Staff," *Library Journal* 22:381 (April, 1897)

21. *Ibid.,* p. 382.

CAROLYN WOOD SHERIF

Professor of Psychology at The Pennsylvania State University in University Park, graduated from Purdue University with highest distinction in 1943. She has been pursuing social psychology and high honors ever since. University appointments include posts at the University of Oklahoma and its Medical School and Cornell University. She has coauthored several books with her husband Muzafer Sherif. Her Orientation in Social Psychology *is in press as of 1975 (Harper and Row).*

Dr. Sherif earned her master's degree in psychology at the University of Iowa and her Doctor of Philosophy Degree in psychology, with a minor in sociology, at the University of Texas.

CAROLYN W. SHERIF

DREAMS AND DILEMMAS
OF BEING A WOMAN TODAY

Many of the dreams and the dilemmas of being a woman today have been personal and real to me. One way to introduce some of them is to introduce myself.

I am a social psychologist. I am one of around 150 women in this country who identified themselves as social psychologists in a recent survey by the American Psychological Association. I am one of the small minority of Ph.D.'s in this country who are women. Within that minority, I am among the 42 percent who are married and have children. Of all full professors in this country, I am one of some 9 percent who are women. As of 1970, I was among the 4 percent of females in this country who earned $10,000 or more a year, and that included all of those rich widows (Bird, 1970).

To escape the morass of categories and percentages in which I have sunk, let me add that I have pursued work as a social psychologist for thirty years, twenty-eight of these in collaboration with my husband, Muzafer Sherif, a social psychologist. Two of our daughters are currently working in libraries, one of them completing the M.L.S. degree at Rutgers.

This personal information is sufficient to establish the fact that in many ways I am an exception. An exception to what? An exception to many of the still prevalent stereotypes about women, or what Walter Lippman called "pictures in the head" in his book on *Public Opinion* (1965). Such "pictures in the head" may or may not reflect the ways women and men behave and feel in actuality. Whether they do or not is really not the point. The salient question is whether such pictures in the head affect us, and whether they affect what happens between men and women.

Most of us, being educated and enlightened citizens of the late twentieth century, will declare, if asked, that we are not governed by stereotypes, that our perceptions of one another are not merely pictures in our heads and that, indeed, we are dedicated to perceiving the uniqueness of each individual whose equality of opportunity and potentiality for self-actualization we value. It is startling, therefore, to examine our reactions to individuals who do not fit neatly into prevailing stereotypes—who are "exceptions." Having made a case that I am such an exception, let me imagine some possible reactions to what I have said so far:

Well, she can't complain. She's shown that a woman can make it in a profession and in the academic world, at that. Why doesn't she tell all the other women to stop griping and get down to work?

What a competitive woman—dead set on success—an aggressive female to the core. We're probably in for an ego trip; all she's talked about is herself. What has she *done* after all? Women teachers are a dime a dozen—unfortunately for our educational system.

Just because she's made it doesn't mean she has anything to say about women. We can't all be super-women. Anyway, she's admitted that she's worked with her husband: she probably wouldn't *be here* without him. What *else* do you suppose she used to get promoted to full professorship?

We can laugh at these imaginary monologues because they are familiar. We too seldom pause to savor the irony that such reactions to the exceptional case are singular and convincing evidence that, in fact, we are governed by stereotyped images of women. Exceptional cases do not lead us to question the pictures in our head. They arouse impulses to alter the case, to embroider it or downgrade the person through stereotyped aspersions, or, if our admiration is won, to elevate the person to a pedestal reserved for those possessing capacities beyond the ken of us mere mortals. By obtuse logic, the exception confirms that our views are, on the whole, correct.

The tenacity of our assumptions in dealing with the exception recalls the story of a man who became convinced that he was dead. His family offered every possible evidence to the contrary, but at last took him to a psychiatrist. The psychiatrist also tested his belief, to no avail. Almost despairing, the psychiatrist thought of an ultimate test. "Listen," he asked, "do dead men bleed?" "No, of course not," replied the man. The psychiatrist seized the man's hand and pricked it with a letter opener. "You see, you bleed! You can't be dead." The man stared at the blood as though he could not believe his eyes. "What do you know," he muttered. "Dead men *do* bleed!"

It is my theme that stereotyped pictures in the head govern our expectations about how women *will* behave, *should* feel and *ought* to act. They are the stuff that expectations and dreams are made of, whether these concern the sexes, dominant and subordinated groups in a society, or other nations and peoples. They are reflections of major arrangements for relations between the sexes, among groups, among nations and peoples. Above all, they reflect the efforts of those with the most powerful influence, and clever persuasiveness to maintain the existing arrangements—in the family, in education, in work, in community and political life.

Our dreams—our very selves—are permeated with their images. Our dilemmas arise as we find that actual living, actual families, real work, day-to-day interaction between the sexes, political realities are not in tune with the dreams, nor can they be, for these are all changing. The realities, however, are peopled with others clinging to the pictures in *their* heads, acting and reacting in terms of the images, and too often shaping actualities in ways designed to keep the image vivid and reinforce its frame with barriers, humiliations or punishments for those who forget how the lines are drawn.

It is not my contention that life from day to day is determined entirely by images frozen on canvas and framed in gilt. Daily living

is bounded by starker realities, some of them documented else-
where in this volume. Rather it is my thesis that the pictures of
women that men and women have in their heads are test patterns
affecting their conceptions of themselves and their dealings with
one another. It is pertinent, therefore, to examine research evidence concerning the effects of such stereotypes on our appraisals
of ourselves and of others. I shall also summarize salient findings
from developmental and social psychology about how we get our
dreams and into dilemmas. Finally, I will evaluate the evidence in
the light of our contemporary scene. It is my hope that the discussion will be relevant to women and men working in libraries.
Surely it will, since the growth of the library into a significant
institution in our society since 1887 was accomplished through
major contributions from women, along with the proliferation of
perhaps the most vicious set of all female stereotypes—that of the
woman librarian.

Assumptions about Women

One of the most basic assumptions in our commonsense, naive
psychologizing about human behavior is that people feel and act as
they do because of the "kind of person" they are—because of
their "nature" or "personality" or their "essence." While I
should like to dismiss such a view as typical of only the uneducated
layman, I cannot. Some major theoretical and research models
used by my colleagues in psychology frequently perpetuate such
assumptions.

In keeping with these assumptions, educated men and women in
this country exhibit rather astounding agreement on the nature of
women. Whether they attribute the source of this "nature" to
the "destiny" of biology or the "fate" of upbringing, they are
usually content to use their consensus for the purpose for which it
is designed, namely to argue the inevitability of things as they are.
Recent research on personal characteristics thought to be typical
of males and females reveals the following conclusions:

1. Males and females are accorded quite different natures, with
   associated differences in expectation as to their behavior.

When these traits are also evaluated by the same persons as to how socially desirable or favorable such qualities are, the image of males wins overwhelmingly (Broverman, *et al.,* 1970).

2. When research techniques permit, and as the educational level of respondents increases, the images of males and females overlap, the overlap representing a "humanity" possessed by both. (Seward, 1946; Hartley, 1970; McGillin, 1973).

3. By and large, both men and women accept the stereotyped images of their own sex and the other sex, along with their associated and implied assignment of social roles in home and community.

4. Among middle-class high school and college samples, men's images of women are typically more flexible and overlap more with their notions of "humanity" than do women's images of their own sex (Seward, 1946; Steinman and Fox, 1966; McGillin, 1973).

5. Ratings of masculine and feminine traits by college students and by trained psychotherapists agree in assigning to males a cluster of personal traits that coincides closely with their image of a "healthy adult person," while consigning an image to females that can only be characterized as pathological. While attributing to women a few redeeming, positive traits of the kind that we might concede even to our own worst enemies, both men and women characterized women as tending to be NOT AT ALL resourceful, intellectual, competent or realistic, and as being immature, subjective, emotional, submissive, easily influenced and wracked with inferiority feelings (Broverman, *et al.,* 1970).

6. By middle childhood (ages 8–11) both boys and girls paint a very traditional picture of what women do and are supposed to do, even though their own mothers are working (Hartley, 1970). These images center around the home and marriage. It is important to note that this consensus occurs even among children whose mothers do not stay at home, for it shows us that images of woman's "proper function" are *not* derived

28   *Women in Librarianship*

solely from children's direct dealings with their own mothers, as many major theories of child development would have us believe.

These stereotyped views of women's nature and their "proper" roles permeate my own academic discipline, psychology. In our recent graduate research seminar on psychology and women at The Pennsylvania State University, we surveyed and read original sources on sex differences in behavior, on infant behavior, on socialization, on cognitive and intellectual development, on achievement motivation, on competitiveness, conformity, and alleged male and female "cognitive styles." Our general conclusion was one of shock at the paucity of factual evidence for the stereotypes mentioned. At the same time, we were awed by the facility with which the writers reached conclusions in line with the stereotypes, despite the weak evidence. Earlier, I had read an article by a young Harvard Ph.D., Naomi Weisstein (1971), entitled "Psychology Constructs the Female, or The Fantasy Life of the Male Psychologist." Its central thesis was as follows: "Psychology has nothing to say about what women are really like, what they need and what they want, essentially because psychology does not know " (p. 70). At the time, I thought that Dr. Weisstein was a bit too pessimistic, but now I fear that she may have understated the case. Psychologists are only beginning to become aware that there are important questions on these topics that are worthy of their efforts in research.

I, for one, had anticipated that data from research on human infants might reveal reliable sex differences in behavior occurring so early in development that they suggest some genetically based differences. Indeed, in reading some of the recent books on the psychology of women, such as that by Judith Bardwick (1971), I had been led to believe that such was the case, for example, that female infants *were* more dependent, less active, more attentive to social stimuli, less aggressive, and less persistent in trying to get around barriers than boy babies. (Bardwick even has a chapter on differences in the way the brain works.) Our seminar experience in poring over the evidence disillusioned me.

The *coup de grace* occurred at the meetings of the American Association for the Advancement of Science at the end of December, 1972, in Washington. There I heard Dr. Eleanor Maccoby of Stanford University, editor of a book on sex differences in which these differences in infant behavior were also cited. She declared that most conclusions citing such differences were unwarranted by the evidence. While one can find such conclusions in print made by "experts," the research evidence is very shaky on most reported early sex differences in behavior. Maccoby's critique was particularly impressive to me because she is among those developmental psychologists who have rather consistently sought for differences that might imply genetic links.

As a result of such experiences, I am unwilling, at present, to speculate on the problem of sex-linked determination of behavior in infancy and early childhood. I believe that sexual differentiation is an exceedingly important biological and physiological fact, but I am willing to suspend judgment and await newer and better evidence concerning its effect on behavior, particularly on social behavior in childhood and adulthood. The stereotypes are clearest with regard to social behavior, but it is precisely there that the evidence for genetic bases is weakest.

On the other hand, I am exceedingly impressed with the power of prevailing stereotyped views of the sexes to affect the interpretation of research data. Unfortunately, the opportunity for their impact on individual lives is greatest in those areas of psychology and social science most closely tied to daily life, namely, applied and clinical practice. When this fact is coupled with the widespread use of testing procedures in the clinical and applied areas that are highly susceptible to interpretive bias, we have a situation in which a great deal of sand can be thrown in a great many eyes.

For example, many of the judgments made by psychologists about women's motivations to achieve or their fear of success, about their "cognitive styles" and personalities are based on so-called projective tests (of which the Rorschach Inkblot test is merely the best known). Yet, it has been found that without labels on the test results qualified clinical judges cannot differentiate accurately between the results produced by psychotics or neurotics and those produced by normal people (Little and Schneidman, 1959) or between those by homosexuals and heterosexuals (Hooker, 1957). I think you can see that, as long as this situation obtains, it will be very easy for "experts" to hand down judgments about the unreliability of female character, or to flood the market with reports on how pessimistic and depressed women are immediately before their menstrual periods. Just how this kind of clinical nonsense could have been or can now be taken seriously as evidence for what women should do, their fitness for work or their competence is astounding. Almost all social indicators of seriously disturbed and deviant actions (including suicide, alcoholism, drug addiction and crimes of violence) show males leading the parade in solid phalanx, outnumbering females by two, three or even four to one. Yet no one, to my knowledge, has taken such hard evidence of problem behavior as a sign that men are unfit or unstable.

You will note, of course, that the same people who bring up such indications of female unfitness scarcely ever refer to intelligence test scores or school achievement. The reasons are simple: females perform as well as males by these criteria. Most of the public fuss about improving achievement in school is all about males. Females under sixteen drop out far less often and, when they do, their departure is less often related to poor school performance. Intelligence test scores, achievements scores and school grades are useful only in attempting to predict what kind of "success" males will have in later life. These tests are not even very good at that, especially if the male does not come from a middle- or upper-class background but, by some fortunate turn of events, is able to gain socially rewarded skills.

Intelligence and achievement test scores are of very little value in predicting future success or occupational achievements of women. The reasons are not hard to find. Women frequently settle down as wife, mother, housekeeper, social hostess, and/or work in readily available occupations, usually service of some kind. These roles have zero value on any scale of occupational achievement. They do not correlate with anything but being female. Of the nearly half of the females in this country who work, there is no pretense that the jobs women happen to attain are related to intelligence or achievement test scores. Women take what they can get or think they can get. True, women with responsible jobs are usually bright, often unusually so. But so are many women with no job or doing routine work.

Therefore, it is nonsense to center any objective discussion of women and the world of work around problems as to the nature of women. Such discussion must start with *how the world of work is structured* and the ways and means that are developed to keep the arrangements as they are. Among such ways and means are the pictures of men and women generally maintained in society, and their specific elaboration to suit specific situations.

Pictures in the head about women who work are elaborated around three clearcut areas in which negative evaluation is considered a final answer to any call for change. The first area is competence in the work to be done. There is research showing that performance by women is rated lower than identical or closely similar performance by men, and that both male and female raters make these errors. For example, identical written passages were rated lower when the alleged author was female than male (Goldberg, 1968). Abstract paintings were rated lower in technical competence when the artist was identified as female than when identified as male (Pheterson, Kiesler and Goldberg, 1971). Chairmen of 147 psychology departments judged female applicants for faculty positions as somewhat less able and as suited to a significantly lower academic rank than male applicants, despite the fact that male and female names had been *randomly* assigned to the applications (Fidell, 1970). A committee recently formed as self-appointed guardians of male prerogatives in academia, including Sidney Hook, appears to have engaged in precisely this kind of nonsense when it was organized to prevent the hiring of women from "lowering academic standards."

The second area concerning women and work is sexual, and it is invariably linked to the third, namely neuroticism. This linkage is clearly implied in the general stereotype of women. It is, I believe, a more modern and intellectually acceptable expression of the older ideology of biological inferiority, which serves its purpose better if one can swallow it. Nevertheless, neuroticism does very well indeed for the intended purpose. This area can be illustrated in terms of discussions that I have heard myself about women in graduate school and academic employment. They run like this: A married woman has divided interests that give preference to husband and/or children, thus leading her to erratic and inconsistent decisions (as if every male student or employee were wholeheartedly identified solely with his work and his employer). A single woman is probably neurotic and sexually frustrated, but if she is not, who knows *what* kind of sexual practices she engages in (as if men may not engage in all of these, including "who knows *what*"). Note that these suspicions are directed at the single woman; if she is engaged, the married argument is used. A divorced or widowed woman is probably the highest risk in this peculiar ideology, if my observations are accurate. She is probably a "trouble maker," as I was once told in all seriousness by a dean. Apparently it did not occur to him that the kind of trouble he had in mind suggests some rather severe hangups on the part of some of his male faculty.

Now my point is that, always and everywhere, such arguments about women's competence, sexuality or mental health are advanced to maintain the status quo with respect to women. They are also likely to occur whenever there is competition for traditionally female jobs. It is then argued men will lend stability, dignity, even importance to the erstwhile female enterprise. These are offensive and defensive tactics quite similar to those used by any powers-that-be to put down aspiring applicants who are not powers-that-be—whether the aspirants be blacks, Chicanos, Jews, Catholics, American Indians or women. The drama has its comic aspects, but there is tragedy as well.

The tragedy inheres in the acceptance of the ideology of the powers-that-be by the aspirants themselves. Women accept definitions of themselves as incompetent; they come to see their sexual status as the primary and dominant fact of their entire lives; and they frequently rush to psychotherapists in the belief that the source of the troubled spirit lies wholly within themselves. Furthermore, as several researchers have shown, women who achieve some modicum of success in work are prone to recognize their own "difference" by assigning to the rest of female humanity all of the stereotyped notions that made their own progress so difficult. Successful women are, therefore, often reluctant to work closely with or under other women. How twisted is a scheme of human relations that, in order to maintain itself, produces in the mind and heart of a woman the seeds for destroying the aspirations of others of her own sex. How brain-washed she has been to come to see herself as an acceptable exception among women who are, in her eyes, unworthy of her association or help.

Spinning Dreams and Difficulties in Mixing Them with Reality

Most accounts of the formation of self-identity start with the family and tend to affix rather permanent praise or blame to parental treatment. While believing firmly in the significance of the family as the scene of much early learning, I shall spend comparatively little time on child-parent relationships. I am convinced that the most powerful influences affecting female self-identity are filtered through the family setting, but have their source and their greatest impact outside of the home, namely in schools and other institutions, through the mass media and through age-mates.

In a recent survey of research, Stein and Bailey (1973) found that a wide variety of parent-child patterns in our culture are associated with the development of little girls who see themselves in traditionally feminine terms. Apparently the surest way for a parent to produce an unusually feminine, obedient and conforming girl who lacks independence and personal responsibility is either to smother her with parental warmth or to be highly directive and restrictive. Still another way to produce a completely feminine girl may be a combination of parental neglect and abuse; at least Konopka (1965) reports this combination associated with the strictly feminine activities of bearing unwanted children and prostitution. The young women she studied were highly feminine, dependent, low in self-esteem and highly conventional in their dreams for themselves as women, whatever their experiences.

Such a variety of parent-child patterns associated with femininity that fits the stereotypes is probably not surprising in a society that emphasizes the feminine stereotypes strongly. In fact, Stein and Bailey (1973) offer some evidence that females who strive consistently for achievement in other than domestic and school activities are likely to have parental treatment that deviates considerably from the patterns that the popular literature tells us is modal for bringing up girls. This unconventional parental treatment combines moderate warmth with pressures on the girl in the form of high standards, withholding of nurturance for not meeting them, approval of achievement efforts and punitiveness for lack of responsibility.

While it is customary to seek the roots of both the dreams and dilemmas of being female in early childhood, especially within the family setting, this effort seems to me wasteful when, in fact, practically any family pattern can be associated with them in our society. The intensive focus on parental-child relationships may blind us to the diverse cultural influences outside of the home, and merely reflected within it, that mold our dreams and create dilemmas no matter what our parents have done. Certainly there is very little evidence to support the Freudian theory that the feminine dilemma starts when the little girl learns that she is a girl and feels anatomically deprived because of that recognition.

Awareness of one's identity as male or female is normally firmly established before three years of age; there is no reliable evidence of consistent preference for a sex other than one's own among preschool children. Furthermore, the meanings given such self-categorizations are highly flexible and inconsistent during these years. The inconsistency is illustrated by an incident reported by Ruth Hartley in the course of her research on self-identity when she asked a four-year-old girl, "Are you an American?" "No," she answered. "My father is. I'm a girl."

In fact, a girl's dreams about the future start with some consistency only during the elementary school years. Most girls are content to be girls during these years. They rapidly acquire images of feminine adulthood beyond their homes from mass media, in school and from peers—all of them conventional and idealistic in the extreme. At the same time, there is evidence that little girls of this age actually have, on the whole, greater freedom than boys in their preferences for games, toys, school work, role playing and in the behavior patterns they exhibit. If anything, the evidence suggests that this "middle childhood" period is one of the most intensive learning of the sex role for boys. Punishment from adults and peers accompanies their deviations into feminine interests, activities and behavior, such as failing to exhibit sufficient interest in sports or in displaying presumably feminine reactions such as crying.

In academic tasks girls typically perform as well or better than boys; they expect to perform as well, and their aspiration levels are as high. There is some evidence that girls are more anxious about failure in school than boys, more likely to be cautious in risking failure, and more likely to attribute failure to themselves than are boys of the same ages (Stein and Bailey, 1973). When confronted with an activity in which failure is possible, girls of these ages show as much effort and determination as boys do.

We find in the research literature that, by adolescence, girls' IQ and academic performance level off or decline on the average during the same years that boys' are increasing (Horrocks, 1969). Girls' expectations of successful achievement are lowered. The proportion of female underachievers increases. Their physical performance in running, jumping, hand grip and throwing levels drop dramatically from ages 12–16 while boys' scores are increasing. Girls discard most of the unusual and/or "masculine" choices of occupations they made in earlier childhood to focus on activities conducive to mate catching or preparing for those occupations defined as traditionally feminine or at least offering opportunities for female employment (Seward, 1946; Bird, 1971). It is also during these years that girls in sizeable numbers wish that they were male, if they could have their choice.

What has happened? Clearly the bodily changes and increased growth rate that herald pubescence are a powerful impetus for changing one's conception of oneself as female. Are they solely responsible for the rather unattractive picture I have sketched? The changes I have described sound more like a decline due to aging than growth to adulthood. Physical changes could not be and are not solely responsible for the decline. The girl has witnessed the public images of glamour associated with her sex and has even been a vicarious participant, for example, through the adventures of her Barbie doll. The prepubescent and adolescent girls have this dream of female glamour aimed at attracting males. Circumstances and growth force the developing girl to measure herself against this glittering image and here, indeed, many a problem of feminine identity starts. For, in fact, her world begins to judge her largely in terms of her attractiveness to males, whether she likes it or not, and she defines herself accordingly. While sexuality is certainly important for the male's self-identity, there really can be no comparison with the exclusive focus on sexual attractiveness that a girl is exposed to throughout adolescence and adulthood until menopause. Society says, in effect, this is *it*. But society does not question this criterion, never suggests that a fruitful life is feasible on any other terms, or even that other areas of life count for a woman's happiness and well-being. Women have to discover that there are other areas of living with different criteria than sexual attractiveness, but they must do so at the risk of being consistently reminded they may "lose" in the central arena, or of actually being stigmatized as "unfeminine."

Society's powerful focus on female sexuality is, if anything, reinforced in the prepubescent and adolescent social circle. Growing up is a jar to the self-identity formed in childhood. Both the physiological events and expectations for becoming adult demand alteration in one's self-image from that of childhood. Because such jars and demands are discomfiting to any male or female, the adolescent reacts by turning more and more toward age-mates. There the girl finds others in the same boat as herself, others to admire and emulate, others to compete with, and others with whom to spend time.

Our own research on adolescent girls suggests that the best way to predict what sorts of activities, what concerns and customs most involve girls during this period is to ascertain whom she associates with regularly in and out of school (Sherif, *et al.*, 1973). In fact, this is a fairly accurate way to predict participation in school and outside activities, concern over appearance and clothing, involvement in sports, interaction with boys after school hours and even the evaluation a girl will make of relevant matters when she is not in the presence of her friends.

Recent observations of high school students suggest that their friendship clusters are becoming increasingly heterosexual in membership. It will be interesting to see if this growing tendency will affect the self-images of girls during adolescence. My guess is that, if it does, it will not be in a direction away from traditional femininity and eventual success in capturing a man as the center of one's existence, because such age-mate groups in adolescence are, on the whole, remarkably insulated from outside influences, except those aspects of the larger culture that can be used in pursuit of their own concerns. For the time being, adolescents in our country are remarkably indifferent to direction from adults who might widen the scope of their self-identity. In fact, even in the enlightened college community of Ithaca, New York, the high school is a hotbed of reaction insofar as any alteration of female images is concerned (Farley, 1970). I am aware that the impact of the woman's movement is beginning to be manifested in high schools, but its impact at present is, I believe, on only a tiny minority.

From high school onward, girls' dreams about the future become increasingly focussed on marriage as the goal of adulthood. The goal is covered with romantic haze. Nine times out of ten it has very little to do with marriages that one has observed, such as one's parents. ("It won't be like *that*.") No, the goal is to "be married." Therein lies self-realization, fulfillment, and a host of other good things, including being "taken care of" and material comfort. The immediate rewards for vigorous pursuit of this still distant goal are popularity, recognition and appreciation by males and females of all ages, and especially one's own age.

The closer a girl comes to adulthood, the greater the pressures placed upon her by her friends, who are dropping into marriages like flies, and by adults in home and school. Response to the pressures means eliminating dreams or aspirations that are not in accord with being feminine, with making the feminine choice. Thus we find a peculiar and ironic contrast between male and female development. While boys are pressed into masculinity early in childhood, the social and official pressures on girls to fit the traditional mold actually increase more and more as they approach adulthood.

At the college level we find girls leaving academic and occupational pursuits in droves in order to marry, changing their majors to more "realistic" choices where women's jobs are available and suffering pangs of anxiety if no likely mate is in the offing. When their activities should be expanding to include the kinds of organizational activities and skills that might aid them in future employment, their opportunities and their own willingness to do so are declining. Those few fortunate women who have clear academic and occupational choices typically regard them as secondary to marriage or blindly believe that marriage and their careers are equally possible alternatives that can be pursued by a woman without conflict. And, despite the potentially liberating effects of changes in sexual mores, young women who place the sexual arena at the center of their priorities are easy prey to unscrupulous males who see "woman's liberation" as a golden opportunity for freeloading. Perhaps young men are not to be blamed when they believe the assertions and token actions masquerading as "liberation" for young women whose hearts are playing for keeps. Nor can we blame young women who center their beings on conjugal or quasi-conjugal relationships (which sound as sweet with another name than marriage) when everything and everyone has defined them as a woman's be-all and end-all.

Now I am not here to discredit marriage or to assign to the institution all blame for the problems of young women today. On the contrary, if I were to blame anyone, it would be our educational institutions which, while urging more *sex* education, have scarcely begun to examine the need to educate students on what being married means, what parenthood means (as opposed to "having children"), what women's status and roles actually have been and are, what working means and its relationship to other spheres of life, including the sexual. We have scarcely begun to examine the implications of the facts that more individuals are not marrying, that marriages are breaking up at an unprecedented rate, that more young men and women have doubts about marrying, and that more and more women have to support themselves, sometimes their children as well.

The urgency to find or select an occupation of interest and to become identified with it is confined to males, both in and outside of the educational system. We cannot blame women students who see the choice and pursuit of career as secondary; they are told that this is the case. The educational system does little enough about occupational or career choice for men, and what it does for women is to assume that the problems and situations they will face are identical. In fact, the curriculum presented to both women and men assures that they will *not* be identical. No course or book tells the man that whatever choice of career he makes must be secondary to the plans of a mate or to offspring.

Educational institutions and the academic disciplines are as guilty as any party to the myths surrounding child care and its supposed demand for the undivided attention of a full-time mother and household worker. These myths and the poverty of adequate arrangements for child care outside of the home create more dilemmas for women than notions about female competence. Caught by them, any woman who marries and pursues a career is bound to face conflict sooner or later—unless she is wealthy. The detrimental effects of childhood neglect which are used to support myths about the essential full-time mother were found among children with no parents at all who were kept in overcrowded, understaffed institutions. To my knowledge there is no clear evidence that a healthy childhood requires the attention full time of a single female adult. In fact, children simply did not get that kind of attention from their mothers until about a century ago when The Family was elevated to its present pedestal along with The Mother, who was supposed to stop having notions of gadding about and stay where she Belonged. Yet, both women and men firmly believe, on the whole, that preschool children need the full-time attention of one woman. The myth is even written into law in the form of age restrictions for supporting children in public day-care facilities. It is merely one example of the failure of our educational system to concern itself with the dilemmas women face or its role in creating the dilemmas.

If I seem to have concentrated unduly on marriage and children, it is because they are symbols of the major difficulty that all women share: society defines womanhood primarily by sexual terms, functions, and responsibilities. Whether a woman marries or not, has children or not, this definition creates manifold dilemmas the minute she tries to be something else or do something else. At the same time, guidelines for work and career are set as though those dilemmas did not exist or, quite often, as though the work and the career must be trivial, owing to her womanhood. In either case, the blame for this state of affairs is placed on her womanhood and on her as a person. As far as I know, there are no parallel dilemmas in manhood, as difficult as it may be in this changing, stressful world.

Untangling Dilemmas

The majority of the dilemmas that confront almost every woman today stem from two sources. On the one hand, the dreams to which she subscribes in the course of growing up have their origins in the social arrangements for living that are designed to keep women in their "place." To the extent that she does not, for one reason or another, stay in the designated grooves and that "place," dilemmas are bound to arise. They may keep her in perpetual uncertainty about where she is and where she belongs; they may require at times almost superhuman efforts; and they may, indeed, nearly crush her as a person. On the other hand, as I have suggested, many of the dilemmas arise because a woman lacks the information and the urgency to make real decisions about her life (perhaps because there lurks in her dreams the mythical white horse ridden by a knight who will save and protect her). Thus, as life goes on, a woman may find herself constantly shifting gears, nibbled by little decisions but actually buffeted by circumstances beyond her immediate control.

It is fairly clear that in these changing times one set of solutions to our problems must be dedicated to joint efforts to change the social arrangements which, on the one hand, deprive women of opportunity while, on the other hand, stuffing them with impossible dreams. This is no new suggestion; it is at least two centuries old. In only the last ten years, the revival of the woman's movement has made it possible to speak realistically once again in these terms. For this, every woman today has reason to be grateful. We should not make the mistake of identifying the woman's movement with any one of the many local and national organizations associated with it. A social movement of any kind is much broader than any single group or organization within it. It demonstrates a widespread pattern of expression of discontent with things as they are and of attempts directed toward changing those conditions that breed such discontent (Sherif and Sherif, 1969). Thus, as in any social movement of any kind, there will be leading figures without universal appeal, actions that appear ridiculous to some at a particular time, and many stops and starts in finding directions. The test of a movement is not any of these shortcomings, but of what its varied parts manage to achieve in the way of clarifying the causes of our difficulties and pointing to solutions.

At the very least, the revived woman's movement has created an atmosphere in which women and men can talk about problems in employment, in treatment, and in personal relations which they could not discuss easily before. Witness the symposium sponsored by Rutgers on women in librarianship and the many similar sessions around the country in different fields. Ten years ago such conversations would have been ridiculed out of existence, and few men would have had any interest in them. I believe that the movement has done much more than that. Not only is it achieving changes in specific conditions, but also it is seeking to eradicate the second cause of women's inferior status to which I referred —namely, women's genuine ignorance and their unwitting drift into situations of conflict and uncertainty.

In January, 1963, I gave a talk at a symposium held at Rice University in its semicentennial year on the role of the educated woman and I remarked: "Many of the problems to which I shall refer would be no problems for women if the educative process . . . included awareness of the condition of human males and females in differing periods and in different places. . . . The requirements of the degree seldom include thoughtful inquiry into the status of women, as part of the total human condition. With specific reference to understanding the problems of women, I will, therefore, commend for your reading some of the books on the topic as part of your education, whether you are a woman or a man . . ." (Sherif, 1964). I mentioned several books then available, although unfortunately not Betty Friedan's *Feminine Mystique*, which appeared that year but which I read later. Now there is a rich and growing literature from which to draw, and there are opportunities for academic study.

I emphasized in 1963 the need for women to understand that the roles of women and men, which are necessarily related, were undergoing changes. "There is nothing particularly feminine in being unaware of the changes that occur, and it is certainly not the mark of an educated person. On the contrary, being educated has to do with awareness of change, with awareness of the conditions of human existence in different places and times, and in the ways those conditions affect the human individuals involved. Some of these human beings are women and some are men. The problems of a changing status of women and changing relationships with men will not go away just because we don't know about them." I believe this even more strongly today.

We must learn that many of the dilemmas that we experience as persons are not strictly private events; they are not merely the results of our own shortcomings. They are related to the social arrangements of our lives. By working on those social arrangements we can also do something positive about our private doubts, uncertainties and conflicts. Since for women librarians, arrangements of work are the cause of many problems, I hope that library schools and alumni associations will exercise leadership in study and actions directed toward reconstructing the work arrangements in libraries. In this endeavor, "consciousness raising" activities may be a useful first step, but I do not think they will be sufficient unto themselves. We should learn from the history of such groups (in the form of T-groups or "sensitivity" groups) that there is nothing particularly productive in awareness of personal problems and their sources unless the process leads to action. It is far too easy for such discussions to end merely with casting blame (in this case, typically on men) if their only justification is to identify personal problems. Instead, they should be initiated within the framework of co-operative efforts to *change* relationships. Such efforts should include serious study of the literature on women's status and work. They should include pilot programs undertaken in the spirit of experimentation to try out alternative arrangements of work.

In such efforts it is sometimes said in moments of enthusiasm that the whole problem is very simple: women's problems would go away if men would only change, for it is a man's world. I agree that it is a man's world, but that will not change unless women change too. In my view, putting all the responsibility for change on men is about as informed as the views of women who are eager to disclaim any connection with what they call "Women's Lib" and reveal their ignorance by adding "of course I'm all for equal pay for equal work." Where do they think such concepts as equal pay for equal work came from? From over a century of the woman's movement and its relationship to workers' movements. Similarly, if one examines the history of the woman's movement, one sees that while women spurred, led and worked for advances in women's rights, they worked and achieved in co-operation with men. It is unreasonable and even unthinkable that men will or can change unless women change too.

In this connection, I cannot help adding another contribution of the current woman's movement, namely its drive to pierce the romantic haze to find out what men are really thinking about. It never fails to astound me when I hear of a divorce that occurred because the woman did not know what her husband thought about women working. Doubtless there is a similar haze surrounding men in many work situations. Do women and men at work know what the members of the opposite sex think? I doubt it.

In solving our present and current personal dilemmas, we might do well to adopt an attitude something like the rabbit in the *Pooh* stories. I believe that it was Winnie the Pooh himself who went to the rabbit's hole and asked, "Is that you, rabbit?" And the rabbit replied, "Well, let's pretend it isn't and see what happens." As women, we might well adopt this point of view as a means of re-examining ourselves, of really looking at those we work with, at the world we live in and the world we want to live in. There are great opportunities today for experimentation in homes, in communities, in school and in work settings if we are courageous enough to know our goals, to understand the past, to act and to look to the future and "see what happens."

References

Bardwick, J. M., *Psychology of Women. A Study of Biocultural Conflicts,* (New York: Harper and Row, 1971).

Bird, Caroline, with Sara Welles Briller, *Born Female: The High Cost of Keeping Women Down,* Rev. ed. (New York: David McKay, 1970).

Broverman, I. K., Broverman, D. M., Carlson, F. E., Rosencrantz, P. S., and Vogel, S. R., "Sex-role Stereotypes and Clinical Judgments of Mental Health," *Journal of Consulting and Clinical Psychology,* 34 (1970), 1–7.

Farley, J. T. T., "Women on the March against the Rebirth of Feminism in an Academic Community" (Ph.D. dissertation, Cornell University, 1970).

Fidell, L. S., "Empirical Verification of Sex Discrimination in Hiring Practices in Psychology," *American Psychologist,* 25 (1970), 1094–1097.

Goldberg, Philip, "Are Women Prejudiced against Women?" *Transaction,* 5, no. 5 (April, 1968), 28–30.

Hartley, R. E., "American Core Culture: Changes and Continuities," Chapter 6 in Georgene Seward and Robert C. Williamson (eds.), *Sex Roles in a Changing Society* (New York: Random House, 1970).

Hooker, Evelyn, "Male Homosexuality and the Rorschach," *Journal of Projective Techniques,* 21 (1957), 18–31.

Horrocks, J. E., *The Psychology of Adolescence: Behavior and Development,* 3d ed. (Boston: Houghton Mifflin, 1969).

Konopka, Gisela, *The Adolescent Girl in Conflict* (Englewood Cliffs, N.J.: Prentice Hall, 1966).

Lippmann, Walter, *Public Opinion* (New York: Macmillan, 1965).

Little, K. B., and Schneidman, E. S., "Congruences among Interpretations of Psychological and Anamestic Data," *Psychological Monographs,* 73 (1959), 1–42.

McGillin, Victoria, "Male and Female Perceptions of Feminine and Masculine Behavior" (M.A. thesis, The Pennsylvania State University, 1973).

Pheterson, G. I., Kiesler, S. B., and Goldberg, P. A., "Evaluation of the Performance of Women as a Function of Their Sex, Achievement, and Personal History," *Journal of Personality and Social Psychology,* 19 (1971), 114–118.

Seward, G. H., *Sex and the Social Order* (New York: McGraw-Hill, 1946).

Sherif, C. W., "Woman's Role in the Human Relations of a Changing World," in C. M. Class (ed.), *The Role of the Educated Woman* (Houston, Texas: Rice University, 1964), pp. 29–41.

Sherif, C. W., Kelly, M., Rodgers, L., Sarup, G., and Tittler, B., "Personal Involvement, Social Judgment and Action." *Journal of Personality and Social Psychology,* 27 (1973), 311–28.

Sherif, Muzafer, and Sherif, C. W., *Social Psychology* (New York: Harper and Row, 1969).

Stein, A. H., and Bailey, M. M., "The Socialization of Achievement Orientation in Females," *Psychological Bulletin* 80 (1973), 345–66.

Steinman, Ann, and Fox, D. J., "Male-Female Perceptions of the Female Roles in the United States," *Journal of Psychology,* 64 (1966), 265–76.

Weisstein, Naomi, "Psychology Constructs the Female, or The Fantasy Life of the Male Psychologist," in M. H. Garskof (ed.), *Roles Women Play: Readings toward Woman's Liberation* (Belmont, Calif.: Brooks-Cole, 1971), pp. 68–83.

HERMAN GREENBERG

Personnel Officer for The Free Library of Philadelphia, was able to draw upon more than a dozen years of expertise concerning library personnel practices at The Free Library as a foundation for his symposium presentation entitled "Sex Discrimination Against Women in Libraries." This paper marks Mr. Greenberg's return as a published speaker with library-school associations. An earlier work called "Civil Service and the Selection Process" presented in Tallahassee at an Institute conducted by the School of Library Science, The Florida State University and the Florida State Library appears in Personnel Utilization in Libraries *published in 1970 by the University Library School.*

Following three years in the army as an intelligence analyst, Mr. Greenberg began his career in personnel service for the City of Philadelphia in 1956. In addition to a Bachelor of Science Degree from The Pennsylvania State University he holds a Master of Business Administration Degree from Drexel University.

HERMAN GREENBERG

SEX DISCRIMINATION AGAINST WOMEN IN LIBRARIES

Based upon the evidence provided by a large mass of information, statistical data, employee grievances and litigation which have been reported in recent years, there is no doubt that sex discrimination against women exists. Discrimination against women in libraries, of course, is simply a reflection of the attitudes and conditions which exist in society as a whole. This discrimination against women in libraries is also indicative of the condition of women as employees in many other occupations and professions. Possibly the degree and scope of discrimination is greater in professions and occupations other than in the library field since, at least in terms of numbers, women dominate the library profession.

Occupationally, women are relatively more disadvantaged today than they were thirty years ago. In 1940 women held 45 percent of all professional and technical jobs but in 1967 they held 37 percent. Despite their 37 percent share of all professional and technical jobs, women hold a disproportionately small share of positions in leading professions.

Women by occupation as a percentage of total workers in the following professions are:[1]

	Percent		*Percent*
Librarian	80	Social Scientist	10
Social Worker	60	Scientist	8
Interior Designer	50	Physician	7
Newspaper Reporter	34	Chemist	5
Recreation Worker	33	Lawyer	3
Statistician	33	Physicist	3
Personnel Worker	25	Engineer	1
Commercial Artist	25	Architect	1
Mathematician	10	Federal Judge	1

The National Management Association found in a survey that one-third of the firms it investigated paid women $5 to $15 a week less than men for the same jobs and the same experience.

Sex discrimination against women is both self-defeating and ironic when considered against the background of a predicted "manpower" shortage of middle management talent which will be needed. A director of the McKinsey Company, a consulting firm, predicts that there will be intense competition for women as managers.

Some major industrial enterprises have already begun to develop their womanpower. Honeywell, in its "manpower" development and training program, attempts to identify high-potential men and women managers.

First, Honeywell carefully analyzes each manager. Review is made of jobs held, accomplishments, performance and aspirations. The human resources development representative sits down with the manager and together they develop a plan to prepare him or her for advancement. This plan may involve individual coaching, special assignments, enrollment in company-sponsored courses or in an on-the-job-training reassignment. Honeywell currently has women managers in finance, pricing, advertising, data processing, personnel and so forth. They comprise, however, only 10 percent of Honeywell's total managers.

The New York Telephone Company has instituted a practice of hiring and promoting women to management level positions whenever possible. One of ten managers is now a woman, and the company expects 600 new management positions for women will open during the course of five years. Their college-recruiting program results in the hiring of women at the first level of management who go through a six-month training program in positions such as business or accounting supervisor, programmer trainee, personnel interviewer and group chief operator. An assessment center receives regular reports from each department concerning both male and female candidates for higher levels of management who go through three days of testing and problem solving often leading to promotion for women as well as men.

The climate for the development of equal rights and opportunities in the field of employment for women has, to a great extent, been created by many of the advocates of the women's liberation movement. This relatively small but vocal group of militant women has been the vanguard of a nonviolent revolution. Because of them, ideas and concepts which were foreign to our culture in the recent past have achieved almost universal acceptance. I am not suggesting that I am in full accord with all of the ideas and proposals of the most militant of these advocates, but without them it is unlikely that the small progress which women have already made and apparently will continue to make would have been possible.

This climate of change has made for improvement in the status of women in employment. Admittedly, there is vast room for additional improvement.

The reasons for the discrimination against women in employment are largely cultural. The cultural climate in which we live, in turn, creates attitudes in men and women which, until recently, were accepted without question. I will not attempt to explain the reasons for culturally created bases for discrimination. This explanation can better be made by our behavioral scientists. However, at this point, I should like to stress that women must make many difficult attitudinal changes in themselves before they can succeed in reversing discrimination.

Women cannot simply rely on the various laws and regulations which exist at the state and federal levels. First, they must be aware of the protection provided by these laws. Secondly, they

Finally, it is my impression that a significant number of women, for whatever reason, once they achieve a reasonable degree of success in terms of advancement seem content to remain at a particular level. Although the same observation may be made for some men, relatively speaking, more women than men appear to fall within this category. As a matter of speculation, it might be reasonable to suggest that the females in this category have been culturally conditioned to accept a certain level of achievement and consider that as success and do not consider that rising to or near the top of the organization is an objective for which to strive.

In preparing for this symposium, I decided to interview several women librarians on the staff whom I considered to be outspoken in their views, including at least one female librarian who has had some interest in the women's liberation movement. Although I do not pretend that these women were selected on any statistically valid sampling basis, I did attempt in microcosm to select a cross-section of female librarian staff members. Included in this cross-section was the chief shop steward and member of the executive board of the union composed of professional and technical employees.

Without exception, these female librarians when interviewed could not cite a single case of discrimination against women at The Free Library of which they were aware, and most of these interviewees had long years of service with The Free Library. One of the women interviewed bemoaned the fact that, if there were a higher percentage of male employees, the status, prestige and pay for the profession would be increased.

All of these female interviewees, again without exception, expressed one great area of concern relating to the Civil Service system involving veterans' preference. They all understood that The Free Library has no power or authority to ignore the advantage which veterans have, if they choose to exercise it, in obtaining appointments and in some cases promotions. Veterans' preference sometimes operates in favor of a female when she has served in the armed services. I recall at least one case when I was required to appoint a female because of veterans' preference whom I otherwise would not have selected for appointment. As further evidence the Free Library's nondiscriminatory practices, the Director's Advisory Council, which is composed of the major division chiefs and staff officers (the top-level administrators who advise the Director on policy matters), is evenly divided between males and females.

If my premise that there is no sex discrimination of any consequence at The Free Library is accurate, then you may properly ask how we have arrived at such a happy state. The answer is that we at The Free Library operate under a merit system.

Although the terms "Civil Service" and "merit system" are frequently used synonymously, a merit system may exist without Civil Service law or commission. Conversely, a Civil Service law may provide for the existence of a Civil Service commission, but a true merit system may, in reality, not exist. Such a situation may occur in a jurisdiction dominated by a single political party. Though the term "merit system" is frequently defined as a method of selecting and retaining public employees, the term can appropriately be applied to any type of employer, including those in the private sector. The term is also used to include many other phases of a personnel administration system: promotion, compensation in relation to the character of the job and working conditions. One authority defines a merit system in its broadest sense as "a personnel system in which comparative merit or achievement governs each individual's selection and progress in the service and in which the condition and rewards of performance contribute to the competency and continuity of the service." [2]

A sound merit system should include most of the following provisions:

1. A classification of positions according to duties and responsibilities
2. An adequately staffed and financed personnel system
3. An equitable compensation plan related to the classification system
4. Competitive selection devices (for all positions except those which involve policy-making)
5. A probationary period

6. A performance evaluation program
7. Uniform rules for leave, hours of work and other conditions of employment
8. Provision for promotion by merit
9. An effective training program
10. A system of separations, including those by retirement and dismissal
11. An adequate retirement system
12. Due processs in an appeal procedure

Although no one can claim perfection for the Free Library's and the City of Philadelphia's personnel program, by and large, it is one which maintains its essential integrity. Many problems exist such as training on an unorganized basis and a highly control-oriented central personnel agency. This merit system, with all of its imperfections, however, in my judgment, reduces or eliminates many types of discrimination.

The one major imperfection directly affecting women is the State of Pennsylvania's veterans' preference law. Although theoretically these laws can aid women who have served in the armed forces, they almost invariably operate to the detriment of women. In Philadelphia, with a "certification rule of two," the veterans' preference law is particularly serious, since not only do veterans receive ten points added to a passing score, but also, when referred with a nonveteran, the veteran must be selected. Needless to say, such laws are totally contrary to all merit system principles. Veterans' preference does not apply to promotional procedures.

It will be difficult to change the laws on veterans' preference which receive support from veterans' organizations, but individual women and women's groups, the more militant the better, have the best opportunities for rescinding or at least amending these laws.

Because the city agencies do not have control of many of the important aspects of the personnel administration process, it is practically impossible to discriminate against women or other groups. It is the City of Philadelphia's personnel department which, with the exception of one class, controls the selection and

promotion process. It is the city personnel department which
develops and administers the Civil Service examinations, grades
the examinations and establishes the eligible lists. In addition, with
a "certification rule of two," i.e., the two top eligible only may be
considered for each position to be filled, the library has little
latitude in the selection and promotion process. It is also the
responsibility of the city personnel department to make certain
that all of the city's operating agencies, including The Free Library, strictly adhere to the Civil Service regulations governing the
selection and promotion process as well as all of the other regulations. The city personnel department performs these control functions with zeal. Finally, it is the City Controller and his staff which
audits many of the city personnel department functions.

What protection do those women have who suffer from discrimination in employment based on their sex? There are, of
course, many state statutes which prohibit this type of discrimination. However, the most significant legal constraints against the
practice of sex discrimination in employment are contained in the
Guidelines on Discrimination Because of Sex, Title 29, Labor,
Chapter XIV, Part 1604, as Amended (as of March 31, 1972). These
are federal regulations, and they have the force of law behind
them. For information and interpretations the U.S. Equal Employment Opportunity Commission should be contacted.

The provisions of these guidelines apply not only to employers
but also to labor organizations and to employment agencies.

The commission states that bona fide occupational exceptions
related to sex should be narrowly interpreted. Such labels as
"men's jobs" and "women's jobs" tend to limit equal opportunity
unnecessarily. The commission will oppose the refusal to hire a
woman because of her sex based on various assumptions relating
to sex; for example, the assumption that the turnover rate is higher
for women than for men. The commission will also oppose what
they refer to as the use of stereotypes; for example, the refusal to
hire men for a particular job because of the belief that men possess
a lower degree of digital dexterity than women, or the refusal to
employ women as sales persons because they are not as aggressive
as men. The commission has enunciated the principle that persons

should be considered on the basis of individual capacities and not on the basis of characteristics attributed to one or the other sex.

The guidelines prohibit the refusal to hire a person because of sex as a result of the preferences of coworkers, the employer, clients or customers, except in a case such as where an actor or actress is required.

As you are probably aware, many state laws and regulations governing the employment of women have been promulgated to protect them from physical harm. Many states, for example, limit the weight women may lift, the shifts they may work, the number of continuous hours they may work and so forth. The commission has decided that such laws and regulations are in conflct with and are superseded by Title VII of the Civil Rights Act of 1964. The same is essentially true of state laws and regulations which discriminate between male and female minors when in conflict with the guidelines.

The guidelines deem that an employer is engaged in unlawful employment practice under state law if: (1) it refuses to hire females in order to avoid payment of minimum wages or overtime required by state law, or (2) it does not provide the same benefits for male employees. *Also, the guidelines provide that any state employment laws, such as those requiring special rest and meal periods or physical facilities which are provided to one sex only, are a violation of Title VII.*

If a state law requires that separate rest rooms be provided for employees of each sex, the employer must do so.

Separate lines of promotion and seniority are prohibited if they would adversely affect an employee.

Discrimination against married females is prohibited.

Help-wanted advertisements cannot indicate a preference unless sex is a bona fide requirement for a particular job.

Private employment agencies are prohibited from discriminating on the basis of sex and cannot deal exclusively with one sex, unless the agency limits its services to furnishing employees for jobs for which sex is a bona fide requirement. An employment agency shares responsibility with the employer if a job order containing an illegal sex requirement is knowingly filled.

An employer may not discriminate between men and women with regard to fringe benefits. The higher cost of providing fringe benefits for one of the sexes is not a defense. An employer may not have a pension plan which provides for retirement age based on sex or which differentiates in benefits on the basis of sex.

Pregnant applicants may not be excluded because of their condition. Disabilities caused or contributed to by pregnancy, miscarriage, abortion, childbirth, and recovery therefore are, for all job-related purposes, temporary disabilities and should be treated as such under any health or temporary disability insurance or sick-leave plan available from the employer. The guidelines intend that the employer treat these conditions as any other type of disability with respect to written or unwritten policies.

In addition to the legal strictures against sex discrimination, any library and any other type of organization which believes it has, or does have a problem of sex discrimination, can attempt to reduce or eliminate such discrimination by a plan of affirmative action.

The following is a partial list of suggested guidelines to follow in planning, developing and implementing an affirmative action program in relation to sex discrimination:

1. The library director and top management should declare and periodically reaffirm an explicit equal-opportunity policy in order to gain acceptance and support from all.
2. The library director should assign responsibility and authority for the program to a high-level executive. This official should be prepared to critically assess operations, to disseminate information about the purpose and goals, to arrange for the training of managers and supervisors, and counselors, if any, to encourage any required change.
3. Each supervisor should be required to participate in developing the plan and should be held accountable for its application within his or her work unit. The supervisor should be held responsible for explaining the plan to his subordinates. The application of the plan should be an important factor in evaluating the supervisor's performance.
4. The management of a library should provide for a vehicle

which will permit staff members to raise questions about the implications and purposes of the plan. Opportunity should be provided for employees to express their feelings on an intermittent basis, to provide ideas and to help resolve mutual problems which arise from the plan. This type of communication between representatives of management and the staff will help to improve the implementation of the plan.

5. If a labor organization exists in the library to represent the staff, the collective bargaining agreement should contain a nondiscrimination clause and a statement in support of the plan.

6. The plan should be publicized through all available means including talks, articles in the house organ, bulletin boards, employee manuals and training sessions. Official copies of the plan should be distributed to all present and newly employed staff members—perhaps also to applicants.

7. The plan should be noted in recruiting literature.

8. Management should obtain assistance in the formulation and implementation of the plan from appropriate governmental agencies, women's organizations and behavioral scientists when necessary to achieve a successful program.

Some Personnel Actions

1. Career counseling.
2. Maintenance of a skills inventory.
3. Participation by qualified women on boards and committees concerned with promotions.
4. Maintenance of an exit interview program to determine the reasons for turnover among women.
5. Provision of opportunity for employees to discuss problems and to obtain advice.
6. If possible assist employees who are responsible for children to find day-care facilities.
7. Provide simultaneous training for the person responsible for the plan with persons heading similar plans in other organi-

zations to facilitate the exchange of ideas, techniques and resources.

8. Provide an on-going training program for supervisors.
9. Provide training on such subjects as human relations, sensitivity training and conflict resolution.
10. Evaluate the plan.

In closing I should like to state that the concept of equal opportunity in employment for women is an idea whose time has come. I, for one, look forward to women participating equally with men in all aspects of library work.

Notes

1. House of Representatives, Special Sub-committee on Education of the Committee on Education and Labor, *Discrimination Against Women* (June 17, 1970), p. 130.

2. O. Glenn Stahl, *Public Personnel Administration,* 5th ed. (New York: Harper and Row, 1962).

DISCUSSION

Editors' Note: *At the conclusion of each presentation, the audience wrote questions on cards which were then collected and given to the appropriate speaker to consult before the discussion period. In some instances, similar audience questions were grouped together for a response. In addition to the written questions, there were remarks from the floor.*

Question: How many female deans of library schools are there?

Schiller: The answer is—very few. In 1970, women held only 19 percent of the top positions in accredited library schools throughout the United States. It is important also, to recognize that women's representation in these top level jobs has been sharply reduced during the past two decades; and that this occurred during a period when librarianship received more support than it had ever received before. In 1950, women held 50 percent of the deanship positions. By 1960 this figure dropped to 27 percent, and by 1970 it was reduced even further to 19 percent. This is a rather dramatic change, and it occurred not only in the key positions in the library schools but in other leadership positions as well. For example, in 1950 women held a majority of the state librarian positions, but by

1970 women were in the minority. Yet when we look at the profession overall, we find that women still represent about 80 percent of all librarians. Although women continue to predominate in the profession at large, at the upper levels, they are being wiped out.

Question: Would you comment on Mr. Greenberg's talk, especially on the question of turnover?

Schiller: Mr. Greenberg reported the figures he gathered at The Free Library and concluded that women were more likely than men to leave their jobs. I would question this conclusion. A major fact revealed by studies of turnover in other occupations is that the higher levels of turnover occur at the lower-level jobs. This is true for women and it is true for men. This at least has been the national experience, and this has been substantiated time and time again. This was also the finding of Alice Bryan, who measured turnover for library employees by job level, and found that there was very little difference in turnover between men and women. It was the level of the job, not the sex of the employee, that was the key factor. I think this is very important because attention is often directed to women's so-called lack of career commitment, but the lack of career opportunities is not seen as an issue. Mr. Greenberg told us that 73 percent of the employees at The Free Library were women and, at the administrative level, 56 percent were women. He then suggested that women were probably better represented at administrative levels in The Free Library than in other libraries across the nation. Perhaps they are. But why is it that in all of these libraries, including The Free Library, women are disproportionately underrepresented in administrative positions? What accounts for this? The problem is that the burden of discrimination has not been placed where it belongs, on the institutional factors which create it. Instead, the burden continues to be placed on women themselves, or else discrimination is seen as an individual matter which arises only in isolated instances. Mr. Greenberg reports, for example, that employees at The Free Library were asked if they had ever encountered sex discrimination and none of them reported that they had. Therefore, there had been no discrimination. But the facts demonstrate that there is discrimination, and it is discrimination on an institutional scale. I have received several letters from search committees and others asking me to recommend the names of qualified women who might be considered as candidates for administrative positions. These letters said in effect: "We need someone who is well qualified as a top administrator, and we don't discriminate against women, but there are none to be found." Now there are close to 100,000 women in our profession. Is the apparent scarcity of qualified women due to the lack of available talent? Again, the difficulty is that we have refused to deal with these questions on an institutional basis. We continue to consider discrimination against women either as something which does not exist, attributing women's unequal status to their own lack of career commitment, or as something which occurs only rarely, when overt prejudice comes into play. But that is only one aspect of a much larger issue. This meeting today represents a great step forward because it formally acknowledges an interest on the part of a library school in this major social issue. This is a beginning.

Question: How come I never heard about Dewey and the library school before this?

Schiller: Well, why haven't we? Perhaps we haven't heard about it because we haven't wanted to hear about it. This is something that goes well below the surface. I think that many of us—women as well as men—have felt that women's predominance in librarianship was something like a permanent disability—something the profession lived with but hasn't wanted to talk about. We are only now beginning to recognize how complex discrimination is. It takes subtle forms. And to understand it, we need to examine women's aspirations as well as their actual opportunities to achieve them. One recent study asked male and female library-school students what positions they would like to reach in their library careers. The results showed that a much larger proportion of the men than of the women aimed to reach the top of the profession. The women's aspirations were much lower. But do the library schools perceive this as a problem? Have the library schools met together to examine how discrimination affects their students and their faculty? Has the ALA done anything to confront the problems of discrimination against women in the profession?

They are beginning to think about it, but this needs to be confronted on an institutional scale, not on an individual one. We can't pass this off any longer by saying we can't report any particular cases of discrimination in our own library.

Sherif: First, I want to thank all of you who gave me cards saying how much you enjoyed my remarks this morning and thank those of you who didn't enjoy them for not writing. Although I would not like to take too much time right now, I have some questions that interest me a great deal. I have a feeling that in Anita Schiller's remarks and previous talk you are getting into an area in which you might well spend more time than in exploring the social psychological aspect, no matter how fascinating. So, I'll try to be short. Somebody pull at my skirt if I go on too long. There are clusters of questions here. From the personal and social psychological point of view, one of the most interesting has to do with the insecurity of women, and particularly of students before job experiences, but continuing on to more insecurity about the level of work being done and certainly about going to higher levels. One question touched on remarks of Rutgers faculty members and another mentioned Matina Horner's studies of what she calls the "fear of success."

I hope that I made it clear this morning that there are plenty of reasons why young women and to some extent young men too should feel very uncertain about themselves, particularly in relation to the world of work. I said that we should start discussions about women in librarianship relative to the arrangements made for work *first,* then discuss what kind of people women are; but it's nonetheless generally true that women are prepared in a very poor way for any kind of work. They are also led to believe that in a variety of respects they don't have the capabilities and the emotional stability that are necessary to succeed. And so, why should we really be surprised that they exhibit insecurity and uncertainty, particularly when they're young? Why should we be surprised when, in the face of new opportunities for advancement, they give up?

Now the truth about this is that these are not strictly private problems for each person individually or for each of us as though we work individually. They are problems dealing with the relationships of human beings, both men and women, in the world. So we should start by working on these problems in relationship with other human beings. It's a very constructive first step you are taking in this seminar by just talking about the problems of work and about relations between men and women. It really ought to go on from there. Let's take a school situation: all right, the young women who come in are insecure. What can we do about it? What kinds of experience in education and in work can be provided that will allow people to develop confidence in their abilities? These are questions that must be asked.

Education is not just some sort of dumping ideas into the head or adding new cards to the file. We are really dealing with whole people here. I'm not suggesting psychological counseling. I'm suggesting that in educational work, in occupational spheres and in specific institutional settings it is necessary to experiment together with whole people. If we have insecurity and uncertainty about ourselves in relation to work, then some steps should be taken *together* to do something about it. There are all kinds of alternatives, which I'll be glad to discuss later. I do not think that any ad hoc solution or adding a course here or there is going to help. I think it is going to take the actions of a lot of people working together.

There was a cluster of questions having to do with men disliking women. Related to that was a question about agressive women. that I mentioned, women in managerial roles acting in ways that seem to destroy the aspirations and the confidence of other women, Related to that was a question about aggressive women. There was one concerning specifically hostility toward a male homosexual and lesbians. Now these are all very complicated questions. I don't think that anybody should delude themselves into thinking that the milk and honey of human kindness is going to take care of all the problems that we face in our work or in our relations with each other as males and females. Many of these conflicts come, as I suggested, from historical ideas that reflect certain kinds of arrangements for work and for male and female relationships. We are influenced by them. You've given me some good examples of how we are. That's all I can say in this short period: Yes, we are all "enculturated"; we are all influenced by our past. We can't get away from that. So what do we do meantime?

I think that there are certain things that can be done. If we find a man or a woman who is discriminating on the basis of sex in a flagrant way, there are legal measures that can be taken, I presume. Also, if it's a question of misunderstanding, the arrangement of work should be looked at very objectively.

In response to several questions, I think we have to face the fact that there are some people who are never going to change as long as they live. Our sexual identity starts very early in life. It is so central and we are so unaware of it that, particularly as we get older, it's very hard to change. Now I, on the other hand, am quite willing to change and I think many of you are. So instead of talking about all those nasty people around who are acting like men who hate women or women who hate women, I think we ought to turn our attention to the constructive side.

I will make just one remark about homosexuals and lesbians. I really feel unqualified to discuss the matter, but I think that, in the world of work, the particular form of sexual activity a person chooses is largely irrelevant. I find it ironic in this day and age that there should be so much fear and suspicion attached to sexual activities involving the same sex when by far the greatest social and personal disturbances are still associated with heterosexual activities. While as a social psychologist I have never studied this issue and do not see it as a major one, I think that the efforts of people who have been discriminated against because of their sexual preferences are going to come into the picture. Insofar as such efforts are concerned with the civil and work rights of these people, there is no question in my mind that they should be recognized.

Meanwhile, I think that we are dealing with questions of cultural norms and values that are reacted to with a vengeance by a lot of people who behave very irrationally, both men and women, in confronting specific forms of sexual behavior to which they are unaccustomed and which are undesirable to them. So we are going to have all kinds of counterreactions and I think that it is going to take a long time to change. Conceptions of sexuality and sexual identity are essential in all the issues I have discussed, including issues of work.

What about class status and sex roles? Well, this is related to important things that I should not respond to glibly. I am sorry there was no time to deal with them earlier.

Why do men want to go into libraries? The structure of work hinges around very large economic issues on which I hope Anita Schiller will elaborate. The plain fact is, as I understand it, that we are living in a country in which the work structure has changed. For example, it is not strictly determined by sex. Men and women are interchangeable in many jobs. We no longer have jobs for most of our young people. We have to put almost half of our young people in college to keep them off the job market. Men go into female professions when they find it difficult to get jobs in others. While this may be immediately threatening to some women, particularly, I would suspect, those who have achieved some degree of competence in their profession and probably also the job seeker, I do not see it in the long run as a bad thing. It will not be bad if it makes men and women face the fact that both in work and in their interpersonal relationships of the most formal as well as the most intimate kind, they definitely are linked by the very fact of being together here on this earth.

I think that it's a good thing for men and women to work in libraries. Somebody asked here whether women colleges are better for insecure girls. I'm not convinced that they are at all. I think it is a good idea sometimes for women and men to discuss their problems with members of their own sex, just as it is for members of anything who find themselves in the same boat. When you're in the same boat, it helps to find out what the boat is like and how your tummy's reacting to the waves. But just talking to others in the same boat won't really take care of the whole situation. It won't locate you in the ocean, and it won't get you to port. So, in the long run, both sexes will have to get together. I can't believe that it's a bad thing that men are entering the profession of librarianship in larger numbers, or that you as women want to go to various higher levels of your professional career.

Question: Was there ever a female personnel director in The Free Library of Philadelphia?

Greenberg: The answer is yes. A woman was my predecessor and my boss for approximately five years; she is now the assistant director of one of the large public library systems in the country. Before taking a position as assistant personnel officer at The Free Library, my first two bosses in the field of personnel administration were women. I learned a great deal from my first three bosses; they were all highly competent. I hope I am not discriminating on the basis of sex in carrying out my job, consciously or unconsciously.

Question: Is there a possibility of unconscious discrimination at The Free Library?

Greenberg: Certainly this is possible, but, if it's unconscious, then somebody has to raise it to the consciousness level. There are techniques for doing this, but The Free Library, like many other large public libraries these days, is fighting for its survival and this would absorb tremendous resources.

I should like to speak to the many questions related to the salaries of males and females. The point I was making when speaking about a merit system and a classification plan is that a classification plan requires that employees be paid equally for the same work. Thus, a man who is classed as Librarian III is paid within the same salary range as a woman who is also classed as Librarian III. Therefore, a man and woman at the same level with the same number of years of service will receive precisely the same salary.

One of the reasons I can say The Free Library doesn't practice conscious sex discrimination is that we have very little to do with the selection process. This is handled by the city personnel department; they measure the relative abilities of the applicants who apply for a particular position as best they can on an objective basis. The city personnel department gives a written examination and possibly also an oral examination if it is appropriate to the particular job. We generally try to have at least one or two women on the oral examinations board. Since we have a rule of two in Philadelphia, we can only consider the two top people on a civil service exam for a job if they're both interested. If two women are at the top of the list, we are required to take one or the other. If that's the case, even if we wished to practice discrimination, we couldn't do so. The city personnel department must certify all new appointments and promotions, and if The Free Library attempted to ignore this rule of two, the city personnel department would rightly refuse to certify the appointment.

I was asked a question which I thought I had covered in my talk; apparently I hadn't. The top management of The Free Library is equally divided between males and females. I don't know that it's worthwhile taking the time to enumerate male or female for each kind of position. If they don't get paid precisely the same salary, this is not the library's policy, but rather it is on the basis of their duties and responsibilities in relation to the classification structure. The question of sex does not enter the picture. The classification and pay plan is established and maintained by the city personnel department.

Question: In relation to what you just said, I had asked a specific question based on the current percentages of men and women in top positions that are supervisory or management. I want to know if there is a distinction between supervisory and management; if so, which is higher, and is there any kind of comparison between percentages of men and women in these two gradations?

Greenberg: Compiling these figures in a hurry was quite a difficult job because we don't keep information based on sexual composition of our work force. I took the first-level supervisory class and went up from that level. In other words, I took Librarian III, which is the first full supervisory level, and everything above Librarian III. Using this approach, I established a generic group entitled supervisory-management and tallied the number of men and women in this category of employment.

Question: In your impression are there more women in middle management than upper management in The Free Library of Philadelphia?

Greenberg: Upper management is the Director's Advisory Council, which is fifty-fifty. In middle management, there are more women I suspect, although I don't have this type of information and it's very difficult information to acquire in a limited time. I suspect there are somewhat more female supervisors than there are male supervisors.

Question: I'm interested in knowing about mobility within the institution. How many women actually make it to the upper management level having started off at a lower sublevel as opposed to men who are brought in from the outside at the management level?

Greenberg: I really can't answer your question without the data, and I don't have them, unfortunately.

Kenneth Duchac: I'd like to make a comment about that. I can tell you what it is like in a system such as the Brooklyn Public Library, where the promotional sequence is handled by a promotion board which is set up and composed of members of both the union and of the library. The board examines all people that are recommended for eligibility for promotion so that the choices are made from that list. Currently, our mobility within the system is almost total because of our contract between the library and the union. The number of positions which are exempted from having to come up through the ranks is a very small number of management jobs. In practice, there are only two of us who have been appointed from outside the system in the last four years at the management level.

Question: How many male directors at Brooklyn Public have been brought in from the outside?

Duchac: I guess all of them. I didn't have anything to do with that.

Question: Was this prior to unionization?

Duchac: I couldn't answer that; I don't have that information.

Question: This symposium has a certain peculiar constituency compared with prior alumni symposia, which I think is relevant to the topic. First, I'd like to direct a question to the audience and ask how many people here are having expenses paid by their institution to attend this symposium? [Show of hands.] You will agree that it is the majority? No, it's more likely about half. The constituency shows more females than males, while in the past it used to be about fifty-fifty. The second question I have is how many people here are in managerial positions of some sort? How many of you supervise other librarians, which is different from supervision of nonprofessionals? It appears to be less than 50 percent. I think there's a peculiar age breakdown—but I won't have the temerity to ask about that!

Schiller: We can't go back to past symposia to count up the number of men and women who were in the audience, but it looks as though this one underrepresents the men in our profession. One of the questions submitted earlier asked, "Why are so few men here today, aside from the library school staff and the panel participants?" Another asked: "Is there any significance for the women's liberation movement in the fact that men are conspicuous by their absence today?" I wonder if anybody in the audience would like to comment on this?

Comment: In our library system, some of the men who are in administration could not take the topic seriously.

Comment: I think that this is a prevailing problem. We women are guilty of doing it also, of laughing about liberation in librarianship and not being able to deal with it straight. I think that this is very obvious today and I feel very helpless in dealing with this aspect of the problem.

Comment: Along these lines, one of the important things to complement women's liberation is men's liberation, and it is time for men to start to think about how they impress women. It is very dificult for men to realize the way they go about doing little things to put down women. I can remember one incident in the library school where a woman tried to hold the door open for me and I just started to reach above her hand and hold the door and say, "Oh, no, you're a woman!" I caught myself, however, and went through. But these things are very important and I believe that, although we librarians are worrying about different financial needs, we must make some effort within the institution to raise our consciousness.

Comment: I think the reason why more men aren't here today is because the men feel that this is not a professional topic and it would be wasting a good day's work.

Comment: I think also that it's threatening: I don't think we should feel that it's a waste. There are men on this panel who are uptight about facing us. It would not have been the same had we been in a room discussing blacks or third world people. I don't know why, but any time men have to discuss women, they always throw in various asides. It's a threatening thing to be faced with a group of women who apparently would like to do something about themselves. I think that most of the male librarians who stayed away today should have been here.

Wooster: This is always the problem. You preach a sermon to the audience but you really want it to reach the ones who didn't come to church; it's the standard communication problem. The only thing I can hope is that if and when this symposium is published that gift copies will become available!

Sherif: I should like to add that what you have said is not true only in librarianship. This is also true in my own field. I conducted a Graduate Research Seminar on psychology and women. The seminar was really student initiated. I just helped. Now we are proposing some courses. The reactions that we get from colleagues are astounding. One commented that there really isn't any literature on this subject. It's amazing. He's a psychologist. There's a whole body of literature on sex differences. There are all kinds of studies on various psychological and social problems that have not been treated in terms of male-female relationships before. The reaction is similar, you see. In order for this to become a professional, or academic, or scholarly topic (as the case may be, depending on the field), it is going to take time. And here we who are somehow or other involved in this area, whether as males or females, have a job to do in showing how male-female relationships are an integral part of work relations, of scholarship and of important problems in academic study. It's a challenging, exciting prospect.

Quesion: It amazes me how a simple strategy seems to have been overlooked too frequently in the women's movement and likewise in the library field. I have noticed that when there was a state meeting in Trenton sometime earlier this year and also a political caucus for women last Saturday, their advertisements did not make an appeal to the men who are interested, who want to act like human beings and who want to give women the human dignity they deserve. Why is there no specific appeal made saying that men of good will are invited? I saw an article just recently in a newspaper where the originator of the entire movement, Betty Friedan, said to the women to put aside the notion of women against men, men against women, women hating men, men hating women, and to seek co-operation. That to me seems so elemental that it hardly had to be called to the attention of anyone. How, for instance, has the Black movement advanced? From the very start they had the good sense to use the strategy to seek and employ the aid of those who were white in the community, who marched on Washington with them. Why is it that we who are interested in the women's movement so frequently overlook that obvious strategy? Women who are married here in the group should invite their husbands. Why shouldn't there be a movement where men who are interested in raising the human dignity of women address other men who are trying to help raise the level of women?

Sherif: I think that it should be said right now that there are such opportunities for men. As I noted earlier, I'm not a member of organizations except professional ones, partly because I lead a very busy full life. The National Organization for Women welcomes men. There are some women's groups who do not admit men and do not want men in the audience. They have a variety of reasons. Some of them are temporary, in the very same terms that in the early days, not of the civil rights movement, but of the more recent black movement, blacks themselves were saying they would just as soon their white brothers and sisters did not come to a meeting, that in fact they cannot come. I think that there is a real reason for that; there is a time and a place where we do need to talk to people that are in the same boat as ourselves. And I think we have to respect that. But there are places for men who want to participate and I'm sure you would be welcome.

Question: Mr. Greenberg mentioned job classifications. I think the National Organization for Women just came out with a very interesting statement on jobs. They're not talking only about equal work for equal pay but about equal pay for equal skills. Just who classifies jobs in libraries? What makes it more skillful to supervise a librarian than to tell stories to hundreds of children a week? Just who decides what skills are there? Libraries are very hierarchical organizations, and the rewards go to the people who are supervising the hierarchy and not the people who are performing the services.

Greenberg: The answer to the question is that the classification and pay division of the city personnel department sets up the classification system. They have had substantial help from private consulting firms. One of the major factors, unfortunately or fortunately, depending on one's point of view, is the question of supervision and program responsibility. This is true to a large degree not only of The Free Library but other organizations as well. Supervision is a major classification factor in all kinds of employment including the private sector of the economy. One can recognize expertise or competence in a special field if it's built into the system. It's not built into our system at the moment, although we are working on it and hope that sometime in the not-too-distant future special expertise and competence will be rewarded by special classification and additional money.

Wooster: I think the serious thing is that the woman who spoke thought that the one who tells stories is at least as important as the supervisor.

Greenberg: In a sense yes, but how do you compensate people on the basis of responsibility? The person who supervises the story teller, it seems to me, has more responsibility under any classification scheme of which I have ever heard.

Comment: That's not true for other professions, such as the teaching professions or for doctors and lawyers; they get paid for their skills.

Greenberg: Well, engineering supervisors get paid more than the engineers they supervise; there's no question about that.

Question: I think that some of us are surprised at how much we learned here, although we thought we were quite well informed before we came. I think we learned in ways that were intended and perhaps in ways that were unintended. I think some of the facts that have been presented are really horrendous, but, in a way, I think we have to understand that all of us here are among the privileged in the profession, no matter how difficult our problems have seemed to be. I wonder if we can extend our concern to those people in the library profession who are not professionals and who have in fact been victims of the societal pressures much more than we have been. I'm thinking of women of my age who have never had any college training but upon whom the library with which I'm most familiar rests and without whom it could not function. I wonder if we can think of these people and particularly concern ourselves with the fact that compared with our salaries theirs are really unbelievable. Is there anything that can be done to raise their status in the field?

Greenberg: Again I would like to refer to our situation at The Free Library of Philadelphia. Our staff, all of it up to a certain level, is extremely well paid. Although I don't have the exact dollar figure, our library pages now earn in excess of $3.50 an hour. Our beginning professional librarians start at $10,194 a year. We also have a very well paid subprofessional staff if this is what you're alluding to.

Schiller: I think the question about extending our concern to others who work in libraries besides professionals is a very important one, because discrimination hits all of us up and down the line. In the library where I work, we have an affirmative action committee, and it represents librarians, library assistants and clerical staff. (They object to the terms "subprofessional" and "nonprofessional" and with good reason.) We assembled data on educational backgrounds, and we found that the female library assistants had substantially more education than the male, but that this was not reflected in their job classifications. In other words, their added educational qualifications did not bring them higher pay. This, of course, contradicts the belief that women receive lower salaries than men because they have less education.

But even more interesting was the relationship between librarians and library assistants that was brought out in our meetings. The library assistants pointed out, for example, that they received only fifteen vacation days a year, compared to twenty-four days for the librarians. This struck us in a very personal way, because this was something that none of the librarians on the

committee had ever thought about at all. It seems to me that among
the many positive things to emerge from the current interest in the
status of women is a heightened awareness of inequity. The
woman issue has conveyed deeper understanding of ourselves and
of the conditions in which we work and live.

Comment: I'd like to mention something in view of what was just
said. The library that I'm in is in the middle of fact-finding, which is
the final step in union negotiations. However, whatever the
fact-finder discovers and decides is right will not change the library
board; they don't have to go along with his recommendation. The
reason that we're in this is that the nonprofessional employees
were offered a practically insulting deal—salaries, fringe benefits,
etc. The professionals (four full-time and two part-time) all voted
the contract down in spite of the offer of a $600-a-year increase for
a two-year contract. Of course, the salaries are quite low but,
nevertheless, it was a good raise in this day and age. However, the
six of us banded together and decided to back the clerical workers.
We're doing this not because we're altruistic, but because we feel
that our library may be falling apart at the seams. The clerical staff
has a very low morale and is very disillusioned and upset and feels
it's been insulted for years. We find that we have to rely on its
members very heavily; we also like them very much.

Comment: Most of the discussion here today has really centered
on the kinds of discrimination that take place within a library.
Another kind of discrimination that hasn't been touched on today
takes place particularly in my field of special librarianship. This
depends on what the head of your company or the personnel
people in your company think of librarianship. It is not librarians
discriminating against librarians; this is the business community
and what they think about librarians. The manpower studies of the
University of Maryland have turned up some very revealing
thoughts on the part of the business community about librarians;
their opinion is very low. What's even more discouraging is the low
opinion librarians have of themselves. When you talk about
women in librarianship, one of the things you have to think about is
whether or not you have a high esteem of yourself as a professional

and in what you do. The problem of discrimination against women is a little less important in my mind than the concept of discrimination against the profession by librarians on the inside and others on the outside.

Comment: It's part of the same problem because it's a "woman's field."

Comment: There are many problems in the field of special librarianship; there are problems of women as managers. This is a big point of discussion in the special library field. Women librarians in special libraries are bad managers. Men librarians in the special library field are bad managers. It has to do with the education of librarians, which is a topic I don't want to get into now. But basically, what I'm trying to get at is that the librarians' own impression about what they do is very important. If librarians would think of themselves as managers that would be a very good thing.

Editors' Note: *During the course of the discussion, Irene Gitomer, director of the Madison Township Public Library, New Jersey, came to the microphone with the following story:*

Gitomer: I didn't come up here to ask a question; I came to tell you a horror story that affects all of us and to ask for your advice and assistance. I think we'll all agree that this was a very useful program and a good thing to do. The American Library Association has also thought that this same type of program was a good thing; at least it did last June when it approached the Economic Status, Fringe Benefits and Welfare committee of the Library Administration Division and asked us to mount just such a program at the annual conference in Las Vegas. They said there were unlimited funds available. So we decided to take it on and tentatively had the working title of "Women Now, Women WOW." WOW stood for Welfare of Women in librarianship. I was in charge of recruiting for this program so I went first to Betty Friedan, who I felt would be a good speaker. Since she will be in Israel the week of the conference, she suggested Wilma Scott Heide as an effective substitute. Ms. Heide is national president of NOW and is also a behaviorist. I called her and she was willing to come for just a $100 honorarium plus expenses. I went back to the LAD board only to find out that all the money had somehow evaporated. I was feeling paranoid and thought that maybe it was because of the program. But I have been told on good authority it wasn't just because of the program and the person we picked to speak; it was because money had shrunk all around, and there were priorities ahead of ours. I inquired into the priorities and found that one of them, for instance, was the Building and Equipments section, which is going to put on a symposium on five-year-old library buildings and how well they work. They need the money to pay union men to show their slides of these five-year-old buildings! I've been trying to get through to Bob Wedgeworth, ALA Executive Director, to see if he has any discretionary funds. The other approach I made was to Michelle Rudy, head of the women's task force of the Social Responsibilities Round Table, to ask if the task force had any money. She was able to get $100 and thought she could raise another hundred. I have had a suggestion here today that I call the *Library Journal Hotline* and ask for help. I want, please, two things from you: I want letters immediately to go to Bob Wedgeworth at ALA, and, if you are in sympathy with this program and would like to support it, please send a check to Michelle Rudy. I think it would be a shame if Ms. Heide couldn't come to Las Vegas and speak to librarians because five-year-old buildings were more important than she was!

Question: What if we who are here would like to make a contribution?

Gitomer: I should be most grateful and pass it on to Michelle. I really don't think this is beside the point of this particular meeting, but I apologize for taking up your time with the speakers.

Sherif: I don't think it is either and I'm going to contribute. I think that you ought to be able to do anything in the American Library Association you want. I come from a professional association where women are only about 20 percent of the membership, but things have been happening in the American Psychological Association. So I say go ahead if you want something to happen.

Question: I am curious to know how many people here are members of ALA? Not too many, it appears. About half.

Editors' Note: *A collection was taken, and before adjournment for informal discussion at the Alumni-Faculty club, it was announced that $141.85 had been collected for the ALA conference program on women in librarianship.*

FEDERAL LAWS [1] AND REGULATIONS CONCERNING SEX DISCRIMINATION IN EDUCATIONAL INSTITUTIONS [2] OCTOBER, 1972

Reprinted by permission of the Project on the Status and Education of Women, Association of American Colleges, 1818 R Street, N.W., Washington, D.C. 20009; Bernice Sandler, Director.

	Executive Order 11246 as amended by 11375	Title VII of the Civil Rights Act of 1964 as amended by the Equal Employment Opportunity Act of 1972
Effective date	Oct. 13, 1968	March 24, 1972 (July 1965 for non-professional workers.) (Institutions with 15-24 employees are not covered until March 24, 1973.)
Which institutions are covered	All institutions with federal contracts of over $10,000.[7]	All institutions with 15 or more employees.
What is prohibited [3]	Discrimination in employment (including hiring, upgrading, salaries, fringe benefits, training, and other conditions of employment) on the basis of race, color, religion, national origin or sex. Covers all employees.	Discrimination in employment (including hiring, upgrading, salaries, fringe benefits, training and other conditions of employment) on the basis of race, color, religion, national origin or sex. Covers all employees.
Exemptions from coverage	None.	Religious institutions are exempt with respect to the employment of individuals of a particular *religion* or *religious* order (including those limited to one sex) to perform work for that institution. (Such institutions are not exempt from the prohibition of discrimination based on sex, color and national origin.)
Who enforces the provisions?	Office of Federal Contract Compliance (OFCC) of the Department of Labor has policy responsibility and oversees federal agency enforcement programs. OFCC has designated HEW as the Compliance Agency responsible for enforcing the Executive Order for all contracts with educational institutions. HEW's Office for Civil Rights (Division of Higher Education) conducts the reviews and investigations.	Equal Employment Opportunity Commission (EEOC).[9]
How is a complaint made?	By letter to OFCC or Secretary of HEW.	By a sworn complaint form, obtainable from EEOC.
Can complaints of a pattern of discrimination be made as well as individual complaints?	Yes. However, individual complaints are referred to EEOC.	Yes.
Who can make a complaint? [4]	Individuals and/or organizations on own behalf or on behalf of aggrieved employee(s) or applicant(s).	Individuals and/or organizations on own behalf or on behalf of aggrieved employee(s) or applicant(s). Members of the commission may also file charges.
Time limit for filing complaints [5]	180 days.	180 days.
Can investigations be made without complaints?	Yes. Government can conduct periodic reviews without a reported violation, as well as in response to complaints. Pre-award reviews are mandatory for contracts over $1,000,000.	No. Government can conduct investigations only if charges have been filed.

Pay Act of 1963 ...mended by the Education ...ments of 1972 (Higher Edu-... Act)	Title IX of the Education Amendments of 1972 (Higher Education Act) [13]	Title VII (Section 799A) & Title VIII (Section 845) of the Public Health Service Act as amended by the Comprehensive Health Manpower Act & the Nurse Training Amendments Act of 1971 [18]
1972 1964, for non-professional ...s.)	July 1, 1972 (Admissions provisions effective July 1, 1973.)	Nov. 18,1971
...titutions.	All institutions receiving federal monies by way of a grant, loan, or contract (other than a contract of insurance or guaranty).	All institutions receiving or benefiting from a grant, loan guarantee, or interest subsidy to health personnel training programs or receiving a contract under Title VII or VIII of the Public Health Service Act.[19]
...mination in salaries (includ-...most all fringe benefits) on ...asis of sex. Covers all em-...s.	Discrimination against students or others [14] on the basis of sex.[15]	Discrimination in admission of students on the basis of sex and against some employees.[20]
	Religious institutions are exempt if the application of the anti-discrimination provisions are not consistent with the religious tenets of such organizations. *Military schools* are exempt if their primary purpose is to train individuals for the military services of the U.S. or the merchant marine. *Discrimination in admissions* [16] is prohibited only in vocational institutions (including vocational high schools), graduate and professional institutions; and public undergraduate coeducational institutions.	None.
...and Hour Division of the ...yment Standards Adminis-...n of the Department of	Federal departments and agencies which are empowered to extend financial aid to educational programs and activities. HEW's Office for Civil Rights (Division of Higher Education) is expected to have primary enforcement powers to conduct the reviews and investigations.[17]	HEW's Office for Civil Rights (Division of Higher Education) conducts the reviews and investigations.
...etter, telephone call, or in ...n to the nearest Wage and ...Division office.	Procedure not yet specified. A letter to Secretary of HEW is acceptable.	Procedure not yet specified. A letter to Secretary, of HEW is acceptable.
	Yes.	Yes.
...duals and/or organizations ...wn behalf or on behalf of ...eved employee(s).	Individuals and/or organizations on own behalf or on behalf of aggrieved party.	Individuals and/or organizations on own behalf or on behalf of aggrieved party.
...fficial limit, but recovery of ...wages is limited by statute ...nitations to two years for a ...illful violation and three ...for a willful violation.	Procedure not yet determined.	Procedure not yet determined.
Government can conduct ...dic reviews without a re-...d violation as well as in re-...e to complaints.	Yes. Government can conduct periodic reviews without a reported violation, as well as in response to complaints.	Yes. Government can conduct periodic reviews without a reported violation, as well as in response to complaints.

Can the entire institution be reviewed?	Yes. HEW may investigate part or all of an institution.	Yes. EEOC may investigate part (all of an establishment.
Record keeping requirements and government access to records	Institution must keep and preserve specified records relevant to the determination of whether violations have occurred. Government is empowered to review all relevant records.	Institution must keep and preserv specified records relevant to th determination of whether viola tions have occurred. Governmer is empowered to review all rele vant records.
Enforcement power and sanctions	Government may delay new contracts, revoke current contracts, and debar institutions from eligibility for future contracts.	If attempts at conciliation fa EEOC or the U.S. Attorney Genera may file suit.[10] Aggrieved indivi uals may also initiate suits. Cou may enjoin respondent from er gaging in unlawful behavior, orde appropriate affirmative actior order reinstatement of employee: and award back pay.
Can back pay be awarded?[6]	Yes. HEW will seek back pay only for employees who were not previously protected by other laws allowing back pay.	Yes. For up to two years prior t filing charges with EEOC.
Affirmative action requirements (There are no restrictions against action which is non-preferential)	Affirmative action plans (including numerical goals and timetables) are required of all contractors with contracts of $50,000 or more and 50 or more employees.[8]	Affirmative action is not require unless charges have been filed, which case it may be included i conciliation agreement or b ordered by the court.
Coverage of labor organizations	Any agreement the contractor may have with a labor organization can not be in conflict with the contractor's affirmative action commitment.	Labor organizations are subject t the same requirements and sanc tions as employers.
Is harassment prohibited?	Institutions are prohibited from discharging or discriminating against any employee or applicant for employment because he/she has made a complaint, assisted with an investigation or instituted proceedings.	Institutions are prohibited fror discharging or discriminatin against any employee or applicar for employment because he/sh has made a complaint, assiste with an investigation or institute proceedings.
Notification of complaints	Notification of complaints has been erratic in the past. HEW is proposing notifying institutions of complaints within 10 days. HEW notifies institutions a few weeks prior to investigation.	EEOC notifies institutions of con plaints within 10 days.
Confidentiality of names	Individual complainant's name is usually given to the institution. Investigation findings are kept confidential by government, but can be revealed by the institution. Policy concerning government disclosure concerning investigations and complaints has not yet been issued. The aggrieved party and respondent are not bound by the confidentiality requirement.	Individual complainant's name i divulged when an investigation i made. Charges are not made pu lic by EEOC, nor can any of it efforts during the conciliatio process be made public by th commission or its employees. court action becomes necessary the identity of the parties involve becomes a matter of public recorc The aggrieved party and respo dent are not bound by the co fidentiality requirement.
For further information, contact	Division of Higher Education Office for Civil Rights Department of HEW Washington, D.C. 20201 or Office of Federal Contract Compliance Employment Standards Administration Department of Labor Washington, D.C. 20210 or Regional HEW or DOL Office	Equal Employment Opportunity Commission 1800 G Street, N.W. Washington, D.C. 20506 or Regional EEOC Office

sually the Wage-Hour Divieviews the entire establish-	Yes. HEW may investigate those parts of an institution which receive federal assistance (as well as other parts of the institution related to the program, whether or not they receive direct federal assistance). If the institution receives *general institutional aid*, the entire institution may be reviewed.	Yes. HEW may investigate those parts of an institution which receive federal assistance under Title VII and VIII (as well as other parts of the institution related to the program, whether or not they receive assistance under these titles).
tion must keep and preserve ed records relevant to the ination of whether viola-have occurred. Government powered to review all rele-ecords.	Institution must keep and preserve specified records relevant to the determination of whether violations have occurred. Government is empowered to review all relevant records.	Institution must keep and preserve specified records relevant to the determination of whether violations have occurred. Government is empowered to review all relevant records.
untary compliance fails,[11] ary of Labor may file suit. ved individuals may initiate when Department of Labor ot done so. Court may enespondent from engaging in ul behavior, and order raises, back pay and assess t.	Government may delay new awards, revoke current awards, and debar institution from eligibility for future awards. Department of Justice may also bring suit at HEW's request.	Government may delay new awards, revoke current awards, and debar institution from eligibility for future awards. Department of Justice may also bring suit at HEW's request.
or up to two years for a lful violation and three for a willful violation.	Probably, to the extent that employees are covered.	Probably, to the extent that employees are covered.
ative action, other than increases and back pay, is quired.	Affirmative action may be required *after discrimination is found.*	Affirmative action may be required *after discrimination is found.*
organizations are prohibited causing or attempting to an employer to discriminate e basis of sex. Complaints be made and suits brought t these organizations.	Procedure not yet clear. Any agreement the institution may have with a labor organization can not be in conflict with the non-discrimination provisions of the legislation.	Procedure not yet clear. Any agreement the institution may have with a labor organization can not be in conflict with the non-discrimination provisions of the legislation.
tions are prohibited from rging or discriminating t any employee because he/ as made a complaint, aswith an investigation or in-d proceedings.	Institutions will be prohibited from discharging or discriminating against any participant or potential participant because he/she has made a complaint, assisted with an investigation or instituted proceedings.	Institutions will be prohibited from discharging or discriminating against any participant or potential participant because he/she has made a complaint, assisted with an investigation or instituted proceedings.
laint procedure is very infor-Employer under review may y not know that a violation een reported.	Procedure not yet determined.	Procedure not yet determined.
lentity of a complainant, as s the employer (and union, lved), is kept in strict cone.[12] If court action becomes sary, the identity of the s involved becomes a matter blic record. The aggrieved and respondent are not by the confidentiality re-ment.	Identity of complainant is kept confidential if possible. If court action becomes necessary, the identity of the parties involved becomes a matter of public record. The aggrieved party and respondent are not bound by the confidentiality requirement.	Identity of complainant is kept confidential if possible. If court action becomes necessary, the identity of the parties involved becomes a matter of public record. The aggrieved party and respondent are not bound by the confidentiality requirement.
and Hour Division yment Standards ninistration tment of Labor ngton, D.C. 20210 or Area, or Regional Wage and ur Office	Division of Higher Education Office for Civil Rights Department of HEW Washington, D.C. 20201 or Regional HEW Office	Division of Higher Education Office for Civil Rights Department of HEW Washington, D.C. 20201 or Regional HEW Office

FOOTNOTES

General

1. State employment and/or human relations laws may also apply to educational institutions. The Equal Rights Amendment to the U.S. Constitution, passed by the Congress and now in the process of ratification would, when ratified, forbid discrimination in publicly supported schools at all levels, including students and faculty.

2. Unless otherwise specified, "institution" includes public and private colleges and universities, elementary and secondary schools, and preschools.

3. A bona fide seniority or merit system is permitted under all legislation, provided the system is not discriminatory on the basis of sex or any other prohibited ground.

4. There are no restrictions against making a complaint under more than one anti-discrimination law at the same time.

5. This time limit refers to the time between an alleged discriminatory act and when a complaint is made. In general, however, the time limit is interpreted liberally when a continuing practice of discrimination is being challenged, rather than a single, isolated discriminatory act.

6. Backpay cannot be awarded prior to the effective date of the legislation.

Executive Order 11246 as amended by 11375

7. The definition of "contract" is very broad and is interpreted to cover all government contracts (even if nominally entitled "grants") which involve a benefit to the federal government.

8. As of January 19, 1973, all covered educational institutions, both public and private, must have *written* affirmative action plans.

Title VII of the Civil Rights Act of 1964 as amended by the Equal Employment Opportunity Act

9. In certain states that have fair employment laws with prohibitions similar to those of Title VII, EEOC automatically defers investigation of charges to the state agency for 60 days. (At the end of this period, EEOC will handle the charges unless the state is actively pursuing the case. About 85 per cent of deferred cases return to EEOC for processing after deferral.)

10. Due to an ambiguity in the law as it relates to public institutions, it is

not yet clear whether EEOC *or* the Attorney General will file suit in all situations which involve public institutions.

Equal Pay Act of 1963 as amended by the Education Amendments of 1972 (*Higher Education Act*)

11. Over 95 per cent of all Equal Pay Act investigations are resolved through voluntary compliance.

12. Unless court action is necessary, the name of the parties need not be revealed. The identity of a complainant or a person furnishing information is never revealed without that person's knowledge and consent.

Title IX of the Education Amendments of 1972 (*Higher Education Act*)

(Minority women are also protected from discrimination on the basis of their race or color by Title VI of the Civil Rights Act of 1964.)

13. Final regulations and guidelines for Title IX of the Education Amendments of 1972 have not yet been published. This chart includes information which is explicitly stated in the law, as well as how the law is likely to be interpreted in light of other precedents and developments.

14. The sex discrimination provision of Title IX is patterned after Title VI of the Civil Rights Act of 1964, which forbids discrimination on the basis of race, color and national origin in all federally assisted programs. By specific exemption, the prohibitions of Title VI do not cover employment practices (except where the primary objective of the federal aid is to provide employment). However, there is no similar exemption for employment in Title IX.

15. Title IX states that: "No person . . . shall, on the basis of sex, be excluded from participation in, be denied the benefits of, or be subjected to discrimination under any education program or activity receiving federal financial assistance. . . ."

16. The following are exempted from the *admissions* provision:

Private undergraduate institutions.
Elementary and secondary schools other than vocational schools.
Single-sex public undergraduate institutions. (If public single-sex undergraduate institutions decide to admit both sexes, they will have 7 years to admit female and male students on a nondiscriminatory basis, provided their plans are approved by the Commissioner of Education.)
Note 1. *These exemptions apply to admissions only.* Such institu-

tions are still subject to all other anti-discrimination provisions of the Act.

Note 2. Single-sex professional, graduate and vocational schools at all levels have until July, 1979, to achieve nondiscriminatory admissions, provided their plans are approved by the Commissioner of Education.

17. Under Title VI of the 1964 Civil Rights Act, which Title IX of the Education Amendments closely parallels, federal agencies which extend aid to educational institutions have delegated their enforcement powers to HEW. A similar delegation of enforcement power is expected under Title IX.

Title VII & Title VIII of the Public Health Service Act as amended by the Comprehensive Health Manpower Act & the Nurse Training Amendments Act of 1971

18. Final regulations and guidelines for Title VII and VIII of the Public Health Service Act have not yet been published. This chart includes information which is explicitly stated in the law, as well as how the law is likely to be inerpreted in light of other precedents and developments.

19. Schools of medicine, osteopathy, dentistry, veterinary medicine, optometry, pharmacy, podiatry, public health, allied public health personnel and nursing are specifically mentioned in Titles VI and VIII. Regulations issued June 1, 1972, by the Secretary of HEW specify that *all* entities applying for awards under Titles VI or VII are subject to the nondiscrimination requirements of the act.

20. HEW regulations state: "Nondiscrimination in admission to a training program includes nondiscrimination in all practices relating to applicants to and students in the program; nondiscrimination in the enjoyment of every right, privilege and opportunity secured by admission to the program; and nondiscrimination in all employment practices relating to employees working directly with applicants to or students in the program."

WOMEN IN LIBRARIANSHIP, 1920–1973

Originally compiled November 1970 by the Women's Liberation Task Force of the Philadelphia Social Responsibilities Round Table: Connie Allstetter, Ona Besses, Marian Figlio, Peggy Kelly, Joyce Post, Pamela Thaxter, Joann Volovski.

Revised and updated June 1973 for the American Library Association Social Responsibilities Round Table Task Force on Women by Margaret Myers, Rutgers Graduate School of Library Service, New Brunswick, N.J.; Jennifer Blythin, Bloomfield Public Library, N.J.; and Bonita Dawson, Albany Public Library, N.Y. Updated June 1974 by Margaret Myers and Sara Chrisman.

Reprinted with permission of the Task Force, this bibliography provides a chronological listing of English-language materials on the topic of women in librarianship.

Best, M. S. "Women and librarianship." *Library Association Record* 23:399–409 Dec. 15, 1921
 Author feels that women can bring virtues of sympathy, courtesy, reliability to library work, but their outlook is limited.
Sanders, S. H. "Letter on the preponderance of women in the American library profession." *Wilson Bulletin for Librarians* 8:230–1 Dec. 1933
 Author deplores preponderance of women librarians since he feels they have a less comprehensive grasp of literature

"Should the preponderance of women in the American library profession be considered an evil?" *Wilson Bulletin for Librarians* 8:403–7   Mar. 1934

    Reply to Sanders' letter, which compliments organizing skill and social grace of female librarians

"Tribute to Cleveland and its feminine staff." *ALA Bulletin* 32:203   Mar. 1938

    Praise for high degree of "conscientiousness, special training and professional competence" of staff

"Weaker sex?" *Library Journal* 63:232   Mar. 15, 1938

    Editorial regarding scarcity of qualified candidates for administrative posts

"In reply to 'The Weaker Sex?' " *Library Journal* 63:294–6   Apr. 15, 1938

    Group of letters commenting on editorial listed above

Shilling, M. W. "Women in librarianship." *South African Libraries* 5:186–90   Apr. 1938

Hunt, M. L. "Men vs. women." *Library Journal* 63:342   May 1, 1938

    Author feels women should work for their own advancement; that utmost concern of both men and women should be for the betterment of the profession

Savord, R. "Men vs. women." *Library Journal* 63:342–3   May 1, 1938

    Blames both men and women for sex discrimination in jobs

Taber, F. T. "Men vs. women." *Library Journal* 63:343   May 1, 1938

    States that sex-discrimination evil exists long before library board chooses its man

Lightfoot, R. M. "Further discussion." *Library Journal* 63:438   June 1, 1938

    Points out that men are more represented in administration in all professions; claims prejudice exists towards male librarian's image

"Status of married women." *ALA Bulletin* 32:402   June 1938

    Survey of 70 libraries to determine attitude towards hiring and promoting married women; majority reported placements were according to ability and educational qualifications

Banning, Mrs. M. C. "Women as administrators." *Library Journal* 63:569   Aug. 1938

    Author regrets that sex should influence administrative choice but thinks militant feminist attitude toward condition equally bad

Alvarez, R. S. "Women's place in librarianship." *Wilson Bulletin for Librarians* 13:175–8   Nov. 1938

Supports position that women hold majority of library administrative positions

Munthe, W. "Librarianship—a feminine vocation?" In his *American Librarianship from a European Angle* pp. 155–60, Chicago: ALA, 1939

Random thoughts on the overfeminization of the profession, reflecting many points of view generally true for the 1930's

Kaiser, W. H. "War between the sexes." *Wilson Bulletin for Librarians* 13:336 Jan. 1939

Reply to Alvarez article; author feels that women do not have equal chance for advancement

Stokes, K. M. "Warning—soft shoulders." *Wilson Bulletin for Librarians* 13:470–1 Mar. 1939

Warns women not to expect soft treatment because they are women; they must be librarians first in order to get equality

Cowper, R. S. "Not in our stars." *Library Association Record* 42:166–7 June 1940

Discusses previous articles on status of women; urges women to demand equal pay for equal work, etc.

Liddle, H. "Resigned on marriage." *Library Assistant* 34:67–8 Apr. 1941

States that women do not become unfit for work when married, so they should not be forced to resign

Matthews, Mrs. R. E. S. "Married women librarians." *Library Journal* 66:650–1 Aug. 1941

Discusses how married women suffer much more discrimination than single women in all fields

"Letter to the editor." *Library World* 46:84 Dec. 1943

An opinion that women are being held in lower positions by men supervisors

Library Association. "Royal Commission on Equal Pay." *Library Association Record* 48:56–7 Mar. 1946

States that men and women should be given equal pay for equal jobs; wants to avoid having profession dominated by one sex

Enser, A. G. S. "Shall the misses be masters?" *Library Association Record* 50:124–5 May 1948

Series of statistics presented showing preponderance of women in profession, which author feels is detrimental

Munn, R. "It's a mistake to recruit men." *Library Journal* 74:1639–40 Nov. 1, 1949

Author feels men will secure more attractive positions because governing bodies prefer men

Oboler, E. M. "Men librarians." *Library Journal* 75:66, 98   Jan. 15, 1950

Claims that men make better administrators than women because of various psychological, physiological reasons

Banister, J. R. "Just how right is Mr. Munn?" *Library Journal* 75:141–2, 155   Feb. 1, 1950

Library boards pay a woman less than a man for doing same job

McDonough, E. "Men librarians." *Library Journal* 75:422, 478   Mar. 15, 1950

Argues that delimitation of field into "women's work" and "men's work" is unfortunate, causing suspicion and mistrust

Heathcote, L. M. "Men librarians." *Library Journal* 75:518, 520   Apr. 1, 1950

Claims that women resent inferior type of man entering profession, not men as such

Enser, A. G. S. "Figures and facts." *Library Association Record* 53:14–15   Jan. 1951

Statistics showing how many women as compared to men are in the British Library Association and in ALA

Hintz, C. W. "Personnel administration-discrimination, despotism, democracy." *PNLA Quarterly* 16:15–22   Oct. 1951

Out of 129 respondents, 65.1% feel discrimination exists against females

Vivian, M. E. "Discrimination against women in the professions; a survey of recent literature." *PNLA Quarterly* 16:83–9   Jan. 1952

Mentions research done on discrimination towards women, followed by bibliography on status of women in professions

Bryan, A. I. *The Public Librarian: A Report of the Public Library Inquiry.* New York: Columbia University Press, 1952. 474 pp.

Includes discussion of separate male and female economic and promotional patterns, with women at top in smaller libraries and men at top in larger libraries with higher salaries

Wilden-Hart, M. "Women in librarianship." *Assistant Librarian* 49:78–80   May 1956

Author feels women's inherent faults cause them to be passed over for many awards and opportunities

Lightfoot, R. M., Jr. "In defense of nepotism." *Library Journal* 82:1610–16   June 15, 1957

Urges that each applicant be considered solely on basis of merit

Hamilton, W. J. "American librarianship: some women." *Library Review* 124:238–47   Winter 1957
    Discusses women who he believes were outstanding librarians
Holt, E. C. "Study of Western Reserve University Library School Graduates, 1934–1953." Master's thesis, Western Reserve University, 1957, 29 pp.
Harvey, J. F. "Variety in the experience of chief librarians." *College and Research Libraries* 19:107–10   Mar. 1958
    Study shows higher percentage of male heads with greater variety of experience; married males considered most mobile, single females least mobile
"Fie, if thy name be woman!" *Library Journal* 84:556   Feb. 15, 1959
    Report of *Who's Who of American Women* where editors found only a small number of librarians included
Paulus, M. "Why lady librarians don't get into *Who's Who!*" *Library Journal* 84:1166   Apr. 15, 1959
    Contends most librarians were probably too busy to bother to fill in the questionnaire about who they are and how good they are
Stone, L. H. "Visit to another world." *Library Journal* 84:1350   May 1, 1959
    Asserts that few women will gain wholehearted knowledge of mankind and manners which characterizes a useful librarian
Colton, G. A. "Women administrators." *Library Journal* 84:1712   June 1, 1959
    Argument over who make better administrators fruitless, because this is individual difference and few are good in all areas
Harvey, J. F. "Apply, if thy name be woman." *Library Journal* 84:1712–13   June 1, 1959
    Defends his 1957 study, *The Librarian's Career;* considered women candidates for every vacancy he has had
Haslam, D. D. "Why more men librarians in Britain?" *Library Journal* 84:3084–5   Oct. 15, 1959
    Indicates normal practice until after World War II was to have a woman resign after marriage
Elliott, L. R. "Salute to the vanguard." *Texas Library Journal* 36:7–10   Mar. 1960
    Praises seven women who did solid professional work in the early 1900's in Texas libraries
Simsova, Mrs. S. "Married women in libraries." *Assistant Librarian* 54:130–2   July 1961

Author feels women should not sacrifice personal lives for profession by not marrying

Harvey, J. F. "Advancement in the library profession." *Wilson Library Bulletin* 36:144–7 Oct. 1961

Study shows males in 92% of high-level positions in large academic libraries and 66% in public libraries

Joyce, C. "Suppliant maidens." *Library Journal* 86:4246–9 Dec. 15, 1961

Contends women's work is necessary but not to be taken seriously

Schultz, S. "Remarks on women in theological librarianship; a panel on professional library personnel." In American Theological Library Association. *Summary of Proceedings*, pp. 100–101, Washington, D.C., 1961

Equality hampered because women are barred from ordination, which is required for faculty status

Erlich, M. "Man-to-man talk." *Library Journal* 87:356, 358 Feb. 1, 1962

Author thinks women have the right to be disgusted with male leadership in profession

Goodfleisch, R. "More from Mineola." *Library Journal* 87:358 Feb. 1, 1962

Author wonders why men are entering librarianship and scooping up the best opportunities and salaries when field is so limited

"Survey to be made of part-time jobs for women." *Library Journal* 87:4406–7 Dec. 1, 1962

Announces N.Y.C. study to find opportunities for part-time jobs

Parrott, S. "Analysis of the Biographies of Librarians Listed in *Who's Who of American Women, 1958–59*." Master's thesis, Atlanta University, 1962, 49 pp.

"Cheesecake and charter." *Liaison* 38 June 1963

Claims that the physical attributes of women librarians are increasingly noticed and publicized

Roberson, B. E. "Library trustees and library school directors: what are you looking for?" *PNLA Quarterly* 29:195–7 Apr. 1965

Library school graduate at age 50 offers her success story to prove older women are good potential source of help

Shera, J. M. "A better class of mouse." *Wilson Library Bulletin* 39:677 Apr. 1965

Contends prestige of librarianship diminished during last century due to feminization of the profession

Holden, M. Y. "The status of women librarians." *Antiquarian Bookman* 36:647–8   Aug. 23, 1965
>   Address at 1965 convention of National Women's Party

Moon, E. E. "Tokenism at the top? Women in minority." *Library Journal* 90:4019   Oct. 1, 1965
>   Editorial reacting to Holden's address, stating situation is not so simple

Jordan, R. T. "In defense of women." *Library Journal* 90:5126   Dec. 1, 1965
>   Points out that the 74 members of the Association of Research Libraries have male directors

Shera, J. H. "Kinder, kueche, und bibliotheken." *Wilson Library Bulletin* 40:365   Dec. 1965
>   Points out certain inherent dangers in experimental financial aid program to married women with families who are ready to return to study and work.

Gaines, E. J. "Library education and the talent shortage." *Library Journal* 91:1770–1   Apr. 1, 1966
>   Considers high proportion of women who withdraw from profession for motherhood not good for stable operations; that rapid personnel turnover inhibits solid, long-range programs

Ward, P. L. *Women and Librarianship: An Investigation into Certain Problems of Library Staffing.* London: Library Association, 1966, 59 pp.
>   Study considers female labor force and suggests ways of re-entering profession after break for marriage and family.

"Hiring of married librarians recommended in British study." *Library Journal* 91:2023   Apr. 15, 1966
>   News item summarizing Ward study

"Married women who are also chartered librarians." *Library World* 67:334   May 1966
>   Ward report welcomed because married women librarians have deplored lack of opportunity to obtain employment

Cronin, A. "The second career." *Drexel Library Quarterly* 2:339–44   Oct. 1966
>   Urges library profession to do more to recognize potential of group who want to re-enter field and make adjustments accordingly

"Equal pay in the public library of South Australia." *Australian Library Journal* 15:191   Oct. 1966
Government implements five-year scheme to equate salaries

Drennan, H. T., and Darling, R. L. "The public librarian." In *Library Manpower: Occupational Characteristics of Public and School Librarians,* pp. 1–14. Washington, D.C.: Government Printing Office, 1966

    Median annual earnings 23.6% lower for women than men in 1961

Blankenship, W. C. "Head librarians: how many men? How many women?" *College and Research Libraries* 28:41–8   Jan. 1967

    A survey of administrators in 660 colleges

"A study of 1967 annual salaries of members of the Special Library Association." *Special Libraries* 58:217–54   Apr. 1967

    Most analyses not divided by sex, but mobility profile shows men more able to move for better positions than women

Brisley, M. A. "Cornelia Marvin Pierce: Pioneer in Library Extension." Master's thesis, University of Chicago, 1967, 80 pp.

Wells, S. B. "Feminization of the American Library Profession, 1876 to 1923." Master's thesis, University of Chicago, 1967, 105 pp.

Hooper, J. "Half a librarian is better than none . . ." *Canadian Librarian* 24:338–40   Jan. 1968

    Advocates part-time employment, particularly for women with family who want to stay in profession

Ormsby, A. "For want of a year." *Assistant Librarian* 61:91   Apr. 1968

    British married librarian who must stop working regrets that her experience will not count when she returns later

Ladenson, A. "Fair Labor Standards Act as applied to libraries." *ALA Bulletin* 62:389–401   Apr. 1968

    Prohibition of employers from discriminating on basis of sex in payment of wages for equal work

Seymour, G. M. "Part-time posts for married women." *Library Association Record* 70:134   May 1968

    Laments lack of work for part-time librarians

"Comment." *Assistant Librarian* 61:148–9   July 1968

    Letters stating cases where married women aren't allowed part-time work to qualify them as chartered librarians in Britain

Bradley, G. "Comment." *Library Association Record* 70:186–7   July 1968

    Argues against part-time employment; claims it is not efficient library practice

"Comment." *Library Association Record* 70:213   Aug. 1968

    More letters regarding library profession as possible place for part-time work, but suggesting that this is difficult to obtain

Porter, D. M. "Married women and librarianship." *Assistant Librarian* 61:226–7   Oct. 1968
>   Outlines four problems deterring married women from returning to a full- or part-time job in the profession

Bradley, B. W. "A Study of the Characteristics, Qualifications and Succession Patterns of Heads of Large U.S. Academic and Public Libraries." Master's thesis, University of Texas, 1968
>   Survey of 50 largest public libraries showed 86% headed by males; all of 50 largest academic libraries with male heads

Reynolds, A. L., and King, C. "Why not partnership librarians?" *Bay State Librarian* 58:3–4   Feb. 1969
>   Proposal for administrators to consider two part-time employees to fill one full-time position, particularly for women who wish to remain in field but have small children

"Women in professional library work." *New Zealand Libraries* 32:4–31   Feb. 1969
>   Four sections dealing with N.Z. survey, a discussion on married women returning to work, and need for part-time work as a step in their careers

Reamer, P. "Consider the wife as librarian." *ALA Bulletin* 63:309   Mar. 1969
>   Letter discussing difficulties of recruiting women for the profession and problem of lack of mobility of married women

Schiller, A. R. "Academic librarians' salaries." *College and Research Libraries* 30:101–11   Mar. 1969
>   Results of a poll on salary of one out of every five academic librarians; men's salaries were higher than women's

Schiller, A. R. "Widening sex gap." *Library Journal* 94:1098–2000   Mar. 15, 1969
>   Statistics supporting contention that women librarians likely to become increasingly disadvantaged in relation to men

Sable, A. P. "The sexuality of the library profession: the male and female librarian." *Wilson Library Bulletin* 43:748–51   Apr. 1969
>   Deals with history of male dominance of profession and stereotype characteristics of male and female

Marchant, M. P. "Faculty-librarian conflict." *Library Journal* 94:2886–9   Sept. 1, 1969
>   Argues that the faculty, predominately male, attributes inferior status to librarians, largely female, by transfer of status process; that upper reaches of library staff (male) tend to have faculty status while lower positions don't

Barber, P. "Ladies in waiting." *Synergy* no. 24:22–25   Dec. 1969
    Asks women to become aware, active, and questions why one
is perpetuating inferiority complex by saying one would rather
work under a man
Morrison, P. D. *The Career of the Academic Librarian: A Study of the
    Social Origins, Educational Attainments, Vocational Experience,
    and Personality Characteristics of a Group of American Aca-
    demic Librarians.* ACRL monograph no. 29. Chicago: ALA,
    1969, 165 pp.
    Among many items studied, there are some data classified by sex
Reeling, P. A. "Undergraduate Female Students as Potential Recruits to
    the Library Profession." Ph.D. thesis, Columbia University, 1969,
    239 pp.
    Study of effectiveness of library recruitment whose subjects hap-
pen to be women
Schiller, A. R. *Characteristics of Professional Personnel in College and
    University Libraries.* Research series No. 16. Springfield: Illinois
    State Library, 1969, 118 pp.
    A study of many items; of particular note, salaries of men and
women show wider gap as experience increases
Simpson, R. L., and Simpson, I. H. "Women and bureaucracy in the
    semi-professions." In A. Etzioni, ed. *The Semi-Professions and
    Their Organization,* pp. 196–265. New York: Free Press, 1969
    Explores problem of career commitment among women; argues
that family roles and expectation of discrimination reduce women's
performance
Stone, E. W. *Factors Related to the Professional Development of
    Librarians.* Metuchen, N.J.: Scarecrow Press, 1969, 281 pp.
    Study includes 1956 and 1961 MLS graduates, with some back-
ground information for women in terms of education, experience,
salary and need for continuing education
Darter, P. "One point of view—born a woman." *Assistant Librarian*
    63:42–44   Mar. 1970
    States that women are missing out in British library profession and
need to go out and prove themselves
Murphy, E. D. "Women and blacks: sexual discrimination in the library
    profession." *Library Journal* 95:959   Mar. 15, 1970
    Parallels between blacks' and women's struggle for equal oppor-
tunity
Schiller, A. R. "The disadvantaged majority: women employed in li-
    braries." *American Libraries* 1:345–9   Apr. 1970

Proposes actions by ALA to ameliorate situation of women who, though in majority, are disadvantaged

Wetherby, P. "Librarianship: opportunity for women?" In *16 Reports on the Status of Professional Women*. Pittsburgh: Know, Inc. Apr. 1970

Brief report presented to first conference of Professional Women's Caucus

Detlefsen, E. G., and Schuman, P. "Overdue: women's liberation movement-I." *Wilson Library Bulletin* 44:962, 964, 982   May 1970

Surveys attitudes and stereotypes; indicates ways in which librarians can influence and change acculturated roles

Hathaway, G. W. "Overdue: women's liberation movement-II." *Wilson Library Bulletin* 44:963, 965   May 1970

Urges that women be given information and freedom in their options within and without the institution

Freedman, J. "Liberated librarians: a look at the second sex in the library profession." *Library Journal* 95:1709–11   May 1, 1970

Surveys aspects of, and suggests possible solutions to, the fact of male ascendancy in librarianship

"Discrimination discussed." *American Libraries* 1:644–5   July 1970

Letters commenting on Schiller's article in *American Libraries,* Apr. 1970, with response by Schiller stating that action to overcome obstacles of inequality need not wait for comprehensive research

Detlefsen, E. G. "Women's liberation meeting at the ALA conference." *AB Bookman's Weekly* 46:90   July 20–27, 1970

Describes beginning of task force on women

Forsman, C. "Up against the stacks: task force on status of women in libraries." *Synergy* no. 25:9   July–Aug. 1970

Discusses issues of salary and promotion discrimination, under-representation of women in library education and administration of libraries, need for improved working conditions

Schuman, P. "Status of women in libraries: task force meets in Detroit." *Library Journal* 95:2635   Aug. 1970

Identifies areas of action needed: administrative guidelines, investigation of materials portraying women, discrimination clearinghouse, information services for women

Carpenter, R. L., and Carpenter, P. A. "The doctorate in librarianship and an assessment of graduate library education." *Journal of Education for Librarianship* 11:3–45   Summer 1970

Among many items surveyed is one showing that salaries for men with doctorates are far better at each age level and for each type of position than for women

"SLA salary survey: 1970." *Special Libraries* 61:333–48   July–Aug. 1970

Shows that in all cetegories of survey (job function, subject, highest academic degree) men's salaries clustered above overall mean and women's salaries clustered below mean

"Team employment." *Library Journal* 95:2853   Sept. 15, 1970

Letters in response to Freedman's article in May 1970 *Library Journal*

Gilliam, B. H. "Housewife—librarian." *Library Journal* 95: 3704–5   Nov. 1, 1970

Case of a mother on a part-time job; author laments lack of financial aid to part-time students

American Association of University Women. *Campus 1970: Where Do Women Stand? Research Report of a Survey on Women in Academe.* Washington, D.C.: Dec. 1970

Among many other topics in study, this survey shows women less likely to be head librarians in schools with enrollment over 10,000 and in public institutions; more likely in private schools or with enrollment under 1000

Presthus, R. *Technological Change and Occupational Responses.* Washington, D.C.: U.S. Department of Health, Education, Welfare, 1970 (ED 045 129)

States that avoidance of conflict, order, dependency are common among librarians; that these bureaucratic characteristics are aggravated by the uncertain career commitment common in female occupations

American Library Association. Social Responsibilities Round Table. Task Force on Women. *Newsletter* Vol. 1—1970—

Reports projects of task force and gives general news of women's materials and activities—4 to 6 issues a year

Rothenberg, L., Rees, A. M., and Kronick, D. A. "An investigation of the educational needs of health sciences library manpower: IV. Characteristics of manpower in health sciences libraries." *Bulletin of Medical Library Association* 59:31–40   Jan. 1971

Shows male professionals in survey had highest rates of job and geographic mobility and salaries

Maloney, R. A. "The 'average' director of a large public library." *Library Journal* 96:443–5   Feb. 1, 1971

Study of directors in 26 libraries in 1969, 1950, and 1930, with analyses of age, sex, training, etc., showing fewer number of women in top positions

Hughes, M. "Sex-based discrimination in law libraries." *Law Library Journal* 64:13–22 Feb. 1971
> Survey shows that male head librarians have higher salaries than women, that there is a concentration of males in large law school libraries and administration positions at younger age

Carey, J. T. "Overdue: taking issue with the issues." *Wilson Library Bulletin* 45:593–4 Feb. 1971
> Author feels lack of mobility and childbearing of married women do not advance careers but that their retarded careers cannot be blamed on prejudice

"Overdue: taking issue with 'Taking issue with the issues' of fem librarian's lib." *Wilson Library Bulletin* 45:780–1 Apr. 1971
> Letters in response to Carey article

"ALA salary survey: personal members." *American Libraries* 2:409–17 Apr. 1971
> Discloses salary figures which indicate inequities between men and women

Gerhardt, L. N. "Melvil! Thou shouldst be living." *Library Journal* 96:2567 Sept. 1, 1971
> Editorial introducing issues of women in profession

Cassell, K. A. "The legal status of women." *Library Journal* 96:2600–3 Sept. 1, 1971
> General discussion of federal laws against sex discrimination with some reference to the condition of librarians

Lowenthal, H. "A healthy anger." *Library Journal* 96:2597–9 Sept. 1, 1971
> Call to direct anger at situations which perpetuate inequalities between sexes in the profession

Schuman, P., and Detlefsen, G. "Sisterhood is serious: an annotated bibliography." *Library Journal* 96:2587–94 Sept. 1, 1971
> Contains 116 items covering women's movement, with plea that librarians recognize programming according to sex

Tuttle, H. W. "Women in academic libraries." *Library Journal* 96:2594–6 Sept. 1, 1971
> Urges women to believe in own potential and ability and then develop own career

"Equal employment opportunity: affirmative action plans for libraries." *American Libraries* 2:977–83 Oct. 1971
> Reviews federal legislation and gives suggestions for libraries to implement it; cites ALA resolution on equal opportunity for women

"Women's lib reactions." *Library Journal* 96:3255   Oct. 15, 1971
    Letters in response to Sept. 1 issue on women in profession
"Affirmative action committee for women appointed at CU." *Library Journal* 96:3552–3   Nov. 1, 1971
    University of California at Berkeley library staff charged to develop program to ensure women optimum employment and promotion
Shepherd S. "Sic 'em II." *American Libraries* 2:1140–1   Dec. 1971
    Letter citing leading female librarians in past; calls on women to educate themselves and not be content with subordinate jobs
Schiller, A. R. "Aware: report on women in librarianship." *American Libraries* 2:1215–16   Dec. 1971
    Review of women's representation in top positions shows rapid decline; also reports on affirmative action plans in academe
Kronus, C. L., and Grimm, J. W. "Women in librarianship: the majority rules?" *Protean* 1:4–9   Dec. 1971
    A study of the nature of employment and promotions in a woman's occupation
"Of sex and administration." *Protean* 1:20–31   Dec. 1971
    Six women library administrators give views on changing role of women
Wood, M. S. "Sex discrimination: the question of 'valid grounds.' " *Protean* 1:32–40   Dec. 1971
    Reviews literature on discrimination patterns in libraries
"Making an issue of it." *Protean* 1:54–6   Dec. 1971
    Summary after special issue; details positive action needed
A Report on the Status of Women Employed in the Library of the University of California, Berkeley, with Recommendations for Affirmative Action. Berkeley, 1971, 58 pp. ($2.00 from University Council, Berkeley)
    Documented account of women concentrated at lowest levels with diminishing opportunities for advancement; presents recommendations for changes in hiring, recruitment, training
DeWeese, L. C. "Status concerns and library professionalism." *College and Research Libraries* 33:31–8   Jan. 1972
    Among many factors, sex didn't seem to account for differences in status concerns; however, marital status did
Dunbar, G. "Discrimination in library schools." *American Libraries* 3:113–14   Feb. 1972
    Argues that older women are not given entrance to library schools
Washington Library Association. SRRT Task Force on Status of Women

and Associated Students of University of Washington Women's Commission. "University of Washington Libraries Discrimination Against Women: Preliminary Report." Seattle, Feb. 1972, 11 pp. (mimeographed)

University of Washington Libraries. Office of the Director. "Response to Preliminary Report on University of Washington Libraries' Alleged Discrimination Against Women." Seattle, Mar. 1972, 6 pp. (mimeographed)

Documents disparities in salaries and rank at one academic library and contains reply by director

Rudy, M. "Women." *Library Journal* 97:738–9 Feb. 15, 1972

Outlines background of ALA/SRRT Task Force on Women and areas of concern, with a description of projects

"UC affirmative action report scores sex and job bias." *Library Journal* 97:958 Mar. 15, 1972

Reviews University of California, at Berkeley Library report with evidence of discrimination and recommendations for change

Schiller, A. R. "The origin of sexism in librarianship." *American Libraries* 3:427–8 Apr. 1972

Notion that libraries are peripheral institutions is not due to women but to distorted social condition and outlook; article includes summary of Berkeley Library report on status of women

Bow, R. "Interrupted careers; the married woman as librarian." *Ontario Library Review* 56:76–78 June 1972

Claims that part-time work and more 9-to-5 jobs are needed for mothers so they can continue to climb career ladder and keep in touch with field during childbearing years

Bayefsky, E. "Women and work: a selection of books and articles." *Ontario Library Review* 56:79–90 June 1972

Bibliography of general works on subject as well as short section on women in librarianship and new approaches to work patterns

"The University of Washington Library and femlib." *Wilson Library Bulletin* 46:948 June 1972

Women's group charges that library discriminates against women in personnel practices; director maintains there is no policy of conscious discrimination

"SRRT groups take action on women's rights issue." *Library Journal* 97:2136–7 June 15, 1972

Briefly explains national task-force roster and activities of Boston group

Frarey, C. J., and Learmont, C. L. "Placements and salaries, 1971:

a modest employment showdown." *Library Journal* 97:2154–
2159   June 15, 1972
   This annual survey of MLS graduates reports on preliminary inves-
tigation of sex discrimination in salaries and employment oppor-
tunities
"Affirmative action program implemented at Berkeley." *Library Journal*
97:2326   July 1972
   Mentions changes and corrective policies begun at University of
California
Pottinger, J. S. "The drive for employment equality." *Protean*
2:6–11   Summer 1972
   Explains how HEW insures nondiscriminatory hiring practices and
why affirmative action programs are necessary in some cases
Little, C. "Librarianship: a female profession?" *Michigan Librarian*
38:10–11   Autumn 1972
   Indicates how Michigan library situation reflects national scene
with statistics on top administrative positions; pleads for women to
re-examine own expectations
"LC claims substantial gains on affirmative action front." *Library Journal*
97:3525–6   Nov. 1, 1972
   Claims higher employment of women in GS grades 6 through 18 and
hiring of more women attorneys
Carpenter, R. L., and Shearer, K. D. "Sex and salary survey; selected
statistics of large public libraries in the U.S. and Canada." *Library
Journal* 97:3682–5   Nov. 15, 1972
   Analysis of 1971 data shows median salary for male directors 30%
higher than for women; library expenditures 30% higher under male
directors; beginning professional salaries under male directors 6.5%
higher
"Boston women librarians tackle sexist attitudes and employment prac-
tices." *Bay State Librarian* 61:7   Dec. 1972
   Concerns, activities and future plans described for local task force
Garlick, M. "LAA salary survey, 1971–72: interim report." *Australian
Library Journal* 21:498–502   Dec. 1972
   Results include salary by sex, by qualifications and sex, and by
experience and sex; survey conducted by Library Association of
Australia
Garrison, D. "The tender technicians: the feminization of public li-
brarianship, 1876–1905." *Journal of Social History* 131–159   Winter
1972–73
   Includes many references from 1800's and turn of century not
included in this bibliography

Schuman, P. "Editorial." *Library Journal* 98:199   Jan. 15, 1973
      Introduces various articles on women's materials and concerns
Sassé, M. "Invisible women: the children's librarian in America." *Library Journal* 98:213–17   Jan. 15, 1973
      Lauds notable women leaders and founders of children's services; notes that dictionaries exclude women who are children's librarians, so that their accomplishments are undervalued and unrecognized
Laura X. "Grow your own. . . . Women's History Research Center." *Library Journal* 98:231–34   Jan. 15, 1973
      Pleas for librarians to support activities of unique library collection
Alvarez, R. S. "Profile of public library chiefs: a serious survey with some comic relief." *Wilson Library Bulletin* 47:578–83   Mar. 1973
      This survey of largest public libraries yields a few statistics about women directors; shows movement towards male appointments
Corwin, M. A. "An Investigation of Female Leadership in State Library Organizations and Local Library Associations, 1876–1923." Master's thesis, University of Chicago Graduate Library School, 1973, 89 pp.
"Special series—female librarians." *Tashokan Zasshi* 67:76–90   Mar. 1973
      Japanese articles on problems, work and life of female librarians, female librarians from viewpoint of males and female librarians in the United States and Canada
Cass, F. M. B. "W(h)ither a female profession?" *Australian Library Journal* 22:49–55   Mar. 1973
      Urges changes in education to help women get training in mathematics for increased use of data-processing in libraries. Commentary on article by others in Mar., May, and June 1973 issues
Clubb, B., and Yaffe, P. "Try it, you'll like it." *Canadian Library Journal* 30:96–100   Mar.—Apr. 1973
      Urges women to realize family and career can coexist
"Management: by communication, by objectives, by women." *IPLO Quarterly* (Institute of Professional Librarians of Ontario) 14:113–134   Apr. 1973
      Special issue includes paper, "Woman—her place in the profession" by M. Beckman
"SRRT Task Force on Women serves as job clearinghouse." *Library Journal* 98:1673   Apr. 1, 1973
      Announces roster for women interested in administrative and specialist positions in libraries
DeFichy, W. "Affirmative action: equal opportunity for women in library

management." *College and Research Libraries* 34:195–201   May 1973

Outlines steps for determining status, assessing policies affecting hiring, parental leave and promotion, and strategies to attain managerial positions

Wheeler, H. R. "Placement services in accredited library schools." May 1973. ERIC Document number: ED 078 847   LI 004 382   May 1973

Surveys practices in posting job notices, handling dossiers, word-of-mouth advertising, and discriminatory actions

Frarey, C. , and Learmont, C. L. "Placements and salaries, 1972: we hold our own." *Library Journal* 98:1880–86   June 15, 1973

This annual review includes data on salary differentials between men and women graduates

Cheda, S. "That special little mechanism." (Paper presented to Canadian Library Association annual conference, June 20, 1973, at Mount Allison College)

Outlines myths and barriers women face in the profession as well as suggestions for actions to overcome masculine mystique, which is a device that prevents women from full participation in the library world

U.S. Bureau of the Census. Census of the population: 1970. Subject Reports—Final Report PC (2) —7A Occupational characteristics. GPO, June 1973

Gives median earnings, weeks worked, school years completed, age for men and women librarians from 1970 census (Table 1)

Taylor, M. R. "External Mobility and Professional Involvement in Librarianship; A Study of the Careers of Librarians Graduating from Accredited Library Schools in 1955." Ph.D. thesis, Rutgers University, 1973

Findings show that the librarian who wants to move becomes involved in professional activities to further career; that immobile women are apt to earn less and are older—males earn higher salaries, have more formal education and move more readily from one state to another

"Action on women's lib front: two suits in motion." *Library Journal* 78:2037   July, 1973

Outlines Helen Wheeler's filed charge of discrimination on basis of sex; mentions NOW efforts to suspend tax-free status of universities and foundations until discrimination is ended

"Salary statistics: university and library reports." *Library Journal* 78:2226   Aug. 1973

Shows rank and salary of women concentrated in lower ranks; widest gap between men and women at university level, but this narrows at two-year colleges

Lee, D. L., and Hall, J. E. "Female library science students and the occupational stereotype: fact or fiction?" *College and Research Libraries* 34:265–267 Sept. 1973

Compares group of library school women with general college student norms; both rank similarly in personality

"SRRT Task Force reports on women's job roster." *Library Journal* 98:2502 Sept. 15, 1973

Shows most requests for women employees come from academic libraries; many younger women are interested in administrative positions

"Women's issue." *New Library World* 74 Oct. 1973

Includes articles from women making a contribution to the profession and also trying to deal with questions which relate to women. Pat Ward compares 1963 United Kingdom statistics for women librarians with 1972 statistics

Tarr, S. A. "The status of women in academic libraries." *North Carolina Libraries* 31:22–32 Fall 1973

Surveys factual information in library literature as well as general studies of academic faculty members and myths regarding women workers

"Draft—ALA equal opportunity policy." *American Libraries* 4:560–61 Oct. 1973

Gives statement which ALA Council later approved in Jan. 1974 (with minor changes) to involve association in promoting employment equity

Gaver, M. V. "Women in publishing and librarianship." *AB Bookman's Weekly* 52:1819 ff. Nov. 26, 1973

Compares similarities in the two professions; urges women to qualify themselves for top jobs with administrative background and Ph.D's; urges women at the top to find ways to help other women

"SLA Salary survey 1973." *Special Libraries* 64:594–628 Dec. 1973

Reports same sex bias as in 1970 survey; $12,900 mean annual salary for women only 75% of the $17,200 mean for men. Also reports correlations between age and sex and race and sex

Tucker, S. *A Salary Survey of Colorado Librarians.* Research paper—M.A. in Librarianship. Dec. 1973, 123 pp. (Available for $3.50 from Colorado Lib. Assoc., 2341 S. Josephine, Denver 80210)

Shows men as a group have more experience, education and mobil-

ity than women as a group; however, women who are equal in these
aspects do not earn salaries equal to those of men

Swanick, M. L. S. "Women and the profession." *APLA Bulletin* (Atlantic
Provinces) 37:118–119   Winter 1973

Summarizes points raised by Sherrill Cheda's speech at the Canadian Library Association

"RI Women in Libraries form chapter of ALA SRRT." *RILA Bulletin* 46
no. 2   Jan. 1974

Carpenter, R. L., and Shearer, K. D. "Sex and salary update." *Library
Journal* 99:101–107   Jan. 15, 1974

Shows continuation of differences in salary by sex in public libraries; that male directors earn 30% more than female; that per
capita support and beginning professionals' salaries are better under
male directors

"Ontario college librarians seek faculty benefits." *Library Journal*
99:95–96   Jan. 15, 1974

Charges teaching faculty receive larger salaries and higher benefits
because predominately male; reports that librarians (predominately
female group) file class-action complaint

Gerhardt, L. N. "Of times, changes, and votes." *Library Journal*
99:165   Jan. 15, 1974; *School Library Journal* 99:5   Jan. 1974

Editorial comments on changes in women's library-leadership positions between 1920's and 1970's; claims that motives behind desire
to change image in 1950's and 1960's were never analyzed and that the
denigration of the founders of modern librarianship short-changed the
opportunities of women in field

Heide, W. S. "On women, men, children, and librarians." *Library
Journal* 99:177–181   Jan. 15, 1974; *School Library Journal*
99:17–21   Jan. 1974

Outlines career concerns of women and social pressures affecting
library service

Josephine, Helen. "Serving the unserved majority: the women's resource
librarian." *Library Journal* 99:188–89   Jan. 15, 1974; *School Library
Journal* 99:28–29   Jan. 1974

Discusses projects of Women's History Library and ways local
librarians can provide information for and about women

"Connecticut SRRT Task Force: women's info. explosion." *Library
Journal* 99:724   Mar. 15, 1974

Rundown of activities of new group called Connecticut Women in
Libraries

Frarey, C. J., and Learmont, C. L. *Library Journal* 99:1767–1779   July, 1974
> Reviews 1973 recent graduate placements and salaries, including comparison of those of men and women graduates

Schiller, A. R. "Women in librarianship." In Voight, M. J., ed. *Advances in Librarianship*, v. 4: 103–147. New York, Academic Press, 1974
> A definitive chapter with extensive bibliography describing historical background and current scene regarding status of women librarians, librarianship as a woman's occupation, and characteristics and careers

To Be Published:

U.S. Bureau of Labor Statistics. Library Manpower—A study of requirements and supply. Washington, D.C.: Government Printing Office
> Analyzes present and projected supply and demand of librarians 1970–85; includes some statistics on employment by sex

Wahba, S. "Job satisfaction of librarians: a comparison between men and women"
> Shows that men and women attach the same importance to the need for security and self-esteem and to social needs but that women hold autonomy and self-actualization of lower importance. Also that women are more dissatisfied in all categories

Wahba, S. "Difference between career pay of women and men: a longitudinal study of librarians and teachers pay." (Contact author at Baruch Graduate Center, 257 Park Ave. So., New York, N.Y. 10010)

Newsletters regularly reporting on women in librarianship:

ALA Social Responsibilities Round Table. (Available from Sherrie Bergman Friedman, SRRT Clearinghouse, P.O. Box 330, Bristol, R.I. 02809 $5—ALA member, $3—non-ALA member, $10—institutions)
> Includes news of task force on women's activities along with other SRRT actions

ALA. SRRT Task Force on Women. (Kay Cassell, 150 E. 30th St., Apt. 1F, New York, N.Y. 10016)
> Besides task force activities, includes information on women's materials, job roster, pertinent legislation and women's movement in general

Emergency Librarian, Vol. 1.—1973. (Six issues a year for $2.00 from

Barbara Clubb, 697 Wellington Crescent, Winnepeg, Manitoba R3M
OA7, Canada)

Recent issues have included news on women in Canada, discrimination cases, subject headings on women, research activities, To-
ronto Library School women students, etc.

Connecticut Women in Libraries. (Available from Gretchen Hammer-
stein, SRRT/CWIL, Groton Public Library, Groton, Conn. 06455)

Mostly activity reports of state group, but some general information on women's materials, etc.